Stirring Prose

Stirring Prose

COOKING
WITH TEXAS AUTHORS

Deborah Douglas

TEXAS A&M UNIVERSITY PRESS
College Station

The paper used in this book meets the minimum requirements
of the American National Standard for Permanence
of Paper for Printed Library Materials, Z39.48-1984.
Binding materials have been chosen for durability.

Library of Congress Cataloging-in-Publication Data

Douglas, Deborah, 1952 –

    Stirring prose : cooking with Texas authors / Deborah Douglas. —
1st ed.

        p.   cm.

    Includes bibliographical references and index.

    ISBN 0-89096-829-2

    1. Cookery.   2. Authors, American — Texas.   I. Title.

TX714.D68   1998

641.5 — dc21   98 - 10810

                                                                      CIP

For my teachers

Contents

Acknowledgment

I would like to thank Anita Foster Scott—known in our family as "Teeter Mosquiter"—for her skill and patience during the preparation of the manuscript.

Introduction

There are two reasons why I have no business whatsoever gathering recipes for this cookbook. First, I don't enjoy eating all that much. I eat mainly because I don't like to go hungry. If someone would only invent them, I would gladly swallow pills labeled "Breakfast," "Dinner," and "Supper." That's not to say I don't enjoy good food and cook good food for my family and notice it when someone's gone to the trouble to prepare a nice meal. It's just that there are lots of things that I'd rather think about than food.

Second, the authors who agreed to contribute these recipes are all much more accomplished writers than I am or ever will be. When my words appear near theirs on a page, I feel like I've been writing with one of my front teeth missing. To put it mildly, I am intimidated, and I apologize ahead of time for my lisped remarks about some of the authors.

Despite these serious flaws in my qualifications, I shoved ahead with the project because I believe that Texas writers deserve more limelight than they're accustomed to getting. A Who's Who–type compendium would have been one way to handle the subject, but this would have meant listing dates of birth, graduation from schools, from when to when of teaching appointments, and years that awards were received. Since I do not like to proofread numbers, I hatched the idea of a cookbook. Granted, there are some numbers in the recipes, but not nearly as many as there would have been had I done it the other way. (This is as good a time as any to caution you about taking every number in a recipe as the gospel truth. I warned you fair that I don't like to proofread numbers.)

Another warning: lists of publications appear as the authors themselves provided them, so don't get aggravated because they vary in exhaustiveness.

There's another reason why I thought a cookbook might be a good way to get my brain wrapped around the subject. Trying to define

"Texas writer" is like deciphering an object in the dark: the harder you stare at it, the fuzzier it becomes. In scientific terms, this peculiar phenomenon results from the absence of photoreceptors at the optic disc—simply put, a blind spot that becomes apparent in low light. Whichever way you say it, the truth remains that, if you want a sharp image, you must force yourself to look to the side and allow the object to ease into focus. Similarly, by asking authors to write about something as familiar as their favorite recipes, they were freed from the big toe–digging constraints of having to talk directly about themselves. The resulting off-center reflections are brilliant slices of their personalities and their writing styles.

It is customary for the editor of a cookbook to test all the recipes to make sure that they are edible or at least not harmful to the consumer's health. I began by trying out Larry L. King's remedy for Asian flu. Not only did it not cure the flu, but I woke up with a horrendous headache, trembling hands, bloodshot eyes, churning stomach, and a surly outlook. Out of consideration for the fine folks who sit around me, I skipped church the next morning and seriously considered calling in sick at work on Monday. That misadventure was the beginning and end of my testing of the included recipes. Put another way: eat and drink at your own risk. (Again, I warned you fair.)

Even so, I am immensely proud to offer you this tasteful roll call of some of our state's best authors. As the waitress says after she sets down your chicken fried steak, Y'all enjoy.

Stirring Prose

Judy Alter

Judy Alter has won awards for her
Western novels, short stories,
and juvenile fiction. She is also director
of Texas Christian University Press.

Judy Alter

According to Judy Alter, director at Texas Christian University Press, if you plan to be a writer *and* live a comfortable life, you need one (or, better still, two or all three) of the following: (1) a day job with health insurance and a retirement package, (2) a supportive (literally and figuratively) spouse, or (3) a generous inheritance. The unvarnished reality is that very few authors—some estimates place the number at only a few hundred in the whole country—make a living exclusively by writing. Most authors supplement their income by teaching or editing or working in a bookstore or at a library. So, if not for the money, then for what?

The obvious answer would be a perky "Because writing is so-o rewarding." Minus the perky tone and the extra syllable, Judy agrees that writing is indeed rewarding—in fact, more rewarding than any profession she can imagine—but adds that writing is also a lot of plain hard work. This is particularly true at the end of the day when you are staring at a manuscript that needs a major overhaul. Still, though, she perseveres, because, like my friend who says, "I don't like to fish. I *have* to fish," Judy may not always enjoy writing, but, simply put, she has no choice but to write. And, like all some-time writers, she is hoping for the breakout book that will give her the financial security to join that profoundly fortunate group who write full-time.

Finally, there's the matter of responsibility. As Judy says, "I think my writing is better than many of the manuscripts that come across my desk. I don't write as well as I want to, but I am a good craftsman, and I feel like I have to keep trying to get better." I think anyone who has read her books will take up the chant: "Go, Judy! Go!"

Judy Alter's

CHRISTMAS COFFEE CAKES

My earliest Christmas memories are of the coffee cakes my mother baked each Christmas Eve. She would bake early in the morning, and by the time my brother and I arrived in the kitchen—why was my father never a part of this?—ten or twelve tree-shaped cakes were ready to be decorated with gumdrops, red and green cherries, silver shot, red hots, red sugar, and whatever else entered our fancies.

Mother was quite strict about the decorating: she beat up sugar icing to just the right consistency—a little runny but not too much so—and then dribbled it across the cakes, with strict instructions to us on the order in which decorations had to go on.

Each finished cake was put on a square of cardboard—festively covered with aluminum foil!—and covered with clear wrap. By late morning, we were all off to deliver the cakes, and I think my father became part of the tradition here, though as soon as my brother was old enough to drive, the delivering was left to the two of us.

We had a regular list of recipients, and at every house where we stopped, we were assured that Christmas morning would not be the same without one of Alice MacBain's coffee cakes. And, always, we left the same warning, the one every recipient already knew: don't put it in the oven to warm, because the icing will melt and the decorations all run off. And always, we left with hearty Christmas wishes ringing in our ears.

Basic Coffee Cake Dough

2 pkg. granular yeast
½ cup warm water
1 can condensed milk, plus enough water to make 4 cups
1 scant cup vegetable oil
1 cup sugar

Dissolve yeast in water (add just a pinch of sugar to help the yeast work) and let it rise about five minutes. Mix milk and water, shortening, and sugar. Add dissolved yeast. Stir in enough flour to make a thin batter, the consistency of cake batter. Let this rise in a warm place until bubbles appear on the surface.

Then, to one cup flour, add:

1 tbs. salt
1 heaping tsp. baking powder
1 rounded tsp. baking soda
2 tbs. cardamom (optional)

Also optional: Coat 16 oz. candied citron with flour and mix into batter; if your family hates citron, you can substitute raisins. (Being a purist, I insist on citron, over the howls of my now-grown children, who don't like raisins either!)

Sift into first mixture. Keep adding flour until it is too stiff to stir with a spoon. Knead well. Don't let the dough get too stiff with too much flour or your coffee cakes will be heavy. This dough will keep a week or so in the refrigerator.

To Shape Christmas Tree Coffee Cakes

Roll handful of dough into a log about 4 to 5 inches long and the size of your thumb (maybe a little bigger). Make the next roll a little shorter, and the next, and so on, until you end with a round-shaped piece of dough for the top of the tree. Add a round base for the trunk. Let rise until almost doubled in size.

To Bake

Bake at 375 degrees for 20 minutes or until lightly browned. Cool thoroughly before decorating.

To Decorate an Alter Coffee Cake

Make a basic powdered sugar/butter/hot water icing. Flavor as you like—I use vanilla and almond. Make the icing fairly runny—you want it to drip off the spoon, but not roll off the cake (tricky business, that!).

Line up all decorations before you begin. Put lighter decorations on first—silver shot, etc.—as they are more likely to roll off. You can always smush quartered gumdrops or halved maraschino cherries into the icing.

I suggest any or all of the following: green sugar or red (I like green better); non pareils (those little colored things—sort of multi-colored shot); silver or gold shot, if you can find it; red hots (these are particularly bad about rolling off); halved red and green maraschino cherries; quartered gumdrops; or anything else that strikes your fancy.

Drizzle icing from a spoon over the cake in a back-and-forth motion. Then, *quickly,* apply decorations.

If you want warm coffee cake, heat it from the bottom only.
You can only make coffee cakes if you intend to share them with friends!

BOOKS

After Pa Was Shot. New York: Morrow, 1978; Dallas: E-Heart and Ellen Temple Publishing, 1990.

Luke and the Van Zandt County War. Fort Worth: Texas Christian University Press, 1984.

Thistle Hill. Fort Worth: Texas Christian University Press, 1987.

Mattie. Garden City, N.Y.: Doubleday, 1988.

Elmer Kelton and West Texas: A Literary Relationship. Denton: University of North Texas Press, 1989.

Growing Up in the Old West. New York: Franklin Watts, 1989.

Maggie and a Horse Named Devildust. Dallas: E-Heart and Ellen Temple Publishing, 1989.

Maggie and the Search for Devildust. Dallas: E-Heart and Ellen Temple Publishing, 1989.

Women of the Old West. New York: Franklin Watts, 1989.

Eli Whitney. New York: Franklin Watts, 1990.

Maggie and Devildust—Ridin' High! Dallas: E-Heart and Ellen Temple Publishing, 1990.

Katie and the Recluse. Dallas: E-Heart and Ellen Temple Publishing, 1991.

A Ballad for Sallie. New York: Doubleday, 1992.

Libbie. New York: Bantam, 1994.

Jessie. New York: Bantam, 1995.

Callie Shaw, Stableboy. Austin, Tex.: Eakin Publishing, 1996.

Cherokee Rose. New York: Bantam, 1996.

RODEO! New York: Franklin Watts, 1996.

There She Is—Miss America! New York: Franklin Watts, 1996.

Wild West Shows. New York: Franklin Watts, 1996.

Meet Me at the Fair. New York: Franklin Watts, 1997.

Governor Ann Richards of Texas. New York: Franklin Watts, forthcoming.

Janis Arnold

*Janis Arnold is a novelist
known for her skillful and diverse
storytelling methods.*

Janis Arnold

Janis Arnold and I are members of the same Methodist church in central San Antonio. People who pay attention to such things call our church an old church. There has even been surface fritter about consolidating with a newer—i.e., bigger and more youthful—church a few miles away in the affluent section of San Antonio. So far, though, our church family is managing well enough on its own, and we've stayed put.

Because we are an old church, we cherish our dwindling numbers of young people and strive to offer them most of the benefits that the youth of the newer church have. This means, though, that nearly every able-bodied and willing adult member takes frequent turns teaching Sunday school, sponsoring choir activities, leading Methodist Youth Foundation, teaching Vacation Bible School, chaperoning youth lock-ins, providing snacks, and on and on. For instance, my son chose Janis's husband Steve to be his adult sponsor—we call it Friend in Faith—for his confirmation classes in 1997. Next year, Janis's son will be in the Sunday School class that I teach the years when I don't have a manuscript deadline the following summer.

Janis does her share of the duties, including teaching Sunday school. One Sunday, as I was collecting the offering envelopes, I peeked into her classroom. She was telling the story of Jesus and Zacchaeus, the despised tax collector who was "short of stature" and who climbed a sycamore tree so that he could see Jesus as he passed through Jericho. Janis was using a flannel board with cut-out characters to tell the story. The four- and five-year-old children sat cross-legged in a semicircle, quiet and intrigued, as she created full-bodied people from the two-dimensional paper characters that clung to the flannel board. Through lively, fabricated conversations—the whole story of Zacchaeus is only ten verses—she created distinctive voices and personalities for Jesus and his disciples and the wee little man Zacchaeus. The children were so convinced that these bits of paper were real people that one of the little girls said through puckered lips, "Oh, poor Mr. Disciple. He must be very tired," when one of the cut-out characters refused to stay put on the flannel board.

So she wouldn't break the story's spell, Janis whispered, "Yes, he stayed up very late last night." She patted the character gently and said, "We'll let him lie down right over here so that he can take a little nap." She told the rest of the story in a stage whisper. The children leaned even closer, eager for the next line.

Janis Arnold

AN INHERITED TALENT

Those who have known me best and longest had a good laugh at the news that I had been asked to contribute to a cookbook. "What did you send in, the list of the twelve take-out restaurants closest to your house?" one of my sisters wanted to know.

"I did not," I replied. After their laughter died down, I refused, on general principles, to tell what recipe I had contributed. If either one of my sisters wants to know how to make Mango Mold, she's going to have to buy this book.

No one in my family thinks of me as a cook. Nor, I might add, do we think of my sisters or brother as cooks either. One of our shared characteristics is: We Don't Cook. We do (however) eat, and we eat at the drop of a hat. Anyone who offers to feed us is showered with appreciation. "You made this?" we ask. "Was it hard? I am sure that it was. I mean it tastes so good." At my mother's house, our first stop after clearing her front door is invariably the kitchen. "Hi, Mom, it smells so good in here, what have you cooked?" we ask.

Mother is more or less resigned. I mean, Her Children Don't Cook, but there are lots of other things that we don't do either. I mean, none of us is in jail or anything like that; she could have it worse. "The ability to cook is An Inherited Talent, but the genetic predisposition does appear to skip every other generation," Mother once said. She was speaking in hopeful, wistful tones as she tried to explain to my husband of about ten minutes how none of her daughters can cook and to prepare him for the fact that the best meals of the rest of his life were probably going to be Eaten Out.

Two weeks prior to the wedding, Mother gave us a cookbook as a shower present. "Janis won't use it," she said to her friends as I unwrapped her gift. "Still, every house needs a *Joy of Cooking*." Although Mother knows many of the recipes by heart, she does occasionally consult it when she is visiting.

My mother is ever an optimist and she continues to hope that some of her grandchildren are going to turn out to be her kitchen *compadres*. My son is only five; the jury is still out on him. Unfortunately for my mother's dreams, most of my son's cousins are older than five. And none of them spends much time in the kitchen. Mother blames this on a poor environment. "Those kids could have cooked, more than likely would have," she says, adding, "IF they'd ever seen anyone do it."

Actually, I do cook. And I make it a point to do it in front of my son.

My son loves Mango Mold, which we generally make together. Of course, I didn't invent this recipe. My mother-in-law used to make Mango Mold. All of her friends used to make it. Cappy's Restaurant in San Antonio (where I love to eat) makes a version—only they call it Mango Mousse. Mango Mold is very easy to make; if you like something sweet that you can serve with just about anything (and call salad), you'll probably like it.

Here's what you need to do: Say to your son, "We are going to cook now." Pull a kitchen chair up to the counter and stand your kid up on the chair. Dump three small boxes of Jell-O (real Jell-O with real sugar) into a bowl. Use two orange-flavored Jell-O and one lemon-flavored. Don't use the new flavor, Mango, which tastes funny. Don't use Lime either. It tastes fine, but the color looks funny. Your kid probably won't eat it.

Boil two cups of water. While you wait for the water to boil, your son can dip his finger in and out of the Jell-O and lick the colored sugar. (Omit this step if he has anything contagious and anyone else besides the immediate family plans to eat the Mango Mold.)

After you add the water to the Jell-O, be sure to stir it until all of the powder has dissolved. If you don't stir enough, you will end up with fuzzy-bottom Jell-O. Nobody, not even your dog, is going to like it.

Now comes the sort of hard part. You *have* to have a can of mangoes. Sometimes H.E.B. has lots of them. I usually buy two cans whenever I see mangoes on the shelves, because sometimes H.E.B. will go for a month or so without any cans at all. If the can comes from Mexico, you will find it with the Mexican food. If it comes from Hawaii, you will find it with the Chinese food. Either way, the can of mangoes looks the same, it's blue. This is a regular-size can. Not a big one and not a tiny little one, either. So far as I know, mangoes don't come in any other size can. But I don't spend a lot of time staring at supermarket shelves, so I might be wrong about this.

Dump the mangoes in your food processor. Actually, a blender works better for this step, except that mine, a relic of distant college days, made its last margarita about two years ago, after which it expired in an interesting cloud of smoke and electrical haze. Process the mangoes and one (eight-ounce) package of cream cheese. You can use reduced-fat or even fat-free cream cheese. Then mix that together with your Jell-O/water. Put the whole concoction in a pan, or a mold, or whatever and let it sit in the refrigerator until it is congealed. There you have it, that's all there is to making Mango Mold.

I really can vouch for this recipe. I have made it an uncountable number of times. Except when I deviated from the above procedure, it has never failed. Actually, I have very high hopes for Mango Mold. I am hoping that by judicious use of this recipe, as well as several other equally difficult recipes currently in my repertoire, I just may raise a son who decides that he does (after all) have a mother who cooks.

BOOKS

Daughters of Memory. Chapel Hill, N.C.: Algonquin Books, 1991.
Excuse Me for Asking. Chapel Hill, N.C.: Algonquin Books, 1994.

Carolyn Banks is best known for her
Robin Vaughan mystery series which are set in
the high-stakes world of professional
equestrianism. She is the former editor of
Horse Play magazine and is an
avid horsewoman.

Carolyn Banks

In one chapter of her book, *Bird by Bird: Some Instructions on Writing and Life* (Pantheon, 1994), author Anne Lamotte describes the way she once felt about another writer who was more critically and financially successful than she was. The chapter is entitled "Jealousy." As I read the chapter, the paper on which it was written took on a lead-green tint. Lamotte writes about how devastating this unbidden emotion was, particularly since the other writer also happened to be a friend: "It can wreak havoc with your self-esteem to find that you are hoping for small bad things to happen to this friend—for, say, her head to blow up."

In jealousy's corral is an unwillingness to be helpful. Maybe it's just that some Texas writers feel sorry for me and figure that I need help in the worst way; however, my experience has been that many of them are anything but stingy and tight-lipped. With a few exceptions—write me or call me and I'll be delighted to tell you which ones, even throw in the name of a book-page editor to boot—they have been willing to offer constructive criticism and to share both their time and their trade secrets. Carolyn Banks is a case in point.

I briefly met Carolyn at a conference that she taught a few months before my book was published in October 1995. As soon as she had a chance to read my book, she made sure that it was reviewed (prominently and favorably) in her local newspaper, and she wrote me a letter listing major magazines that might consider reviewing a book like mine. She ended the letter with a peppy paragraph about the importance, these days, of writers being willing to promote their own books. I don't think she singled me out or felt particularly sorry for me. I think Carolyn is genuinely pleased when someone she knows has a bit of success. And I know for sure that she'd never entertain the notion of someone's head blowing up, for goodness sakes.

Carolyn Banks's

OLIVE GROVE PASTA

The first thing you'll want to do is lay in a huge store of salad greens. The recipe doesn't call for salad greens, mind you, but after eating Olive Grove Pasta, you'll want to atone for the number of calories you've consumed by eating salad greens and broth for days afterward. And you'll want to buy them now so you don't have to waddle out to the store.

I'm only half kidding. But get a load of the ingredients for Olive Fettuccine and you'll know why I say "half."

> 1 12-oz. package of cracked black pepper fettuccine. (Exotic as it sounds, you can purchase the Pasta LaBella brand at the H.E.B. in Bastrop. It's expensive, but if you like spicy food, you'll quickly get addicted to this pasta.) If you can't find that, try to get whole-wheat fettuccine. If you can't find that, go for the old stand-by semolina stuff; but DO get fettuccine. You'll want its width as a bearer of the sauce.

Which reminds me, there are additional caveats to issue with this recipe. It calls for LOTS of olives. So if you're serving it to company, you want to make sure that you've ascertained that said folks actually like olives. Otherwise, you'll be in the kitchen making peanut butter sandwiches for the olive haters in the group. Or the ones who don't like spicy food, or the ones on low-calorie or low-sodium (because olives are salty) diets. This is a vegetarian dish, by the way.

So okay. We've got that out of the way. Let's get back to the ingredients:

> 1 12-oz. package of cracked black pepper fettuccine
> 1 10-oz. jar of green olives stuffed with pimento. The Village Park ones labeled salad olives are good because they are less than perfect and, since you'll be chopping them anyway, you may as well buy the cheaper ones.
> 1 3-oz. can of sliced or chopped black olives
> 1 4-oz. bottle of olive oil

1 14-oz. can of Swanson's vegetable broth
1 head of fresh garlic
¼ cup of dried parsley or 2 cups of chopped fresh parsley
1 tsp. of dried oregano
½ tsp. of crushed red pepper
Grated Romano or Parmesan cheese

Okay. While you're cooking the fettuccine (I usually cook it a wee bit less than the label advises, *al dente*), pour the olive oil into a skillet and heat it up. A big cast-iron skillet is best.

Meanwhile, smash some garlic cloves with the broad side of a butter knife (which makes them really easy to peel), chop them up, and toss them into the hot olive oil.

Add half the green olives (5 oz.), drained and mutilated, and the whole can of black olives (also drained). Dump the parsley, oregano, and red pepper in and stir.

When everything is coated with olive oil and really hot, pour in half a can to a cup of the veggie broth, and let it hiss while you test the fettuccine for doneness.

If it's done, drain it and put it back into the pot you cooked it in.

When the veggie broth just starts boiling, pour the mixture over the pasta and mix well. If the skillet you've used for the sauce is big enough, go back and forth to sop up all the oil.

Use one of those claw-like pasta servers, because the olives tend to hide on the bottom and if you don't use a claw, it's conceivable that you will serve an olive-less portion to someone.

Turn up the Puccini, pour some Cabernet Sauvignon (I don't know if that's the best wine to serve. I have it with everything, even apple pie), and *mangia, mangia*. I don't serve side dishes with this, because the olives are so strongly flavored, they would just overpower everything else you might try to offer. A loaf of crusty French bread, though (I like the Earth Grains kind you can heat up in your own oven), is great with it, and great as a pusher and sopper, too.

This, by the way, is a classy dish: earthy and colorful. Eat enough of it, and you too will look, well, earthy at least.

Note: This is an amended version of a recipe which appeared in *Good Housekeeping* magazine in 1992.

BOOKS

Death by Dressage. New York: Fawcett, 1993.
Groomed for Death. New York: Fawcett, 1995.
Murder Well-Bred. New York: Fawcett, 1995.
Death on the Diagonal. New York: Fawcett, 1996.
A Horse to Die For. New York: Fawcett, 1996.

Cindy Bonner

*Cindy Bonner is best known for her
Lily novels, the first of which
was published in 1992.*

Cindy Bonner

In 1994, Cindy Bonner and her family moved to Yorktown, a South Texas town with a population of about 2,500 and only two stoplights— and those revert to blinking after 10 P.M. Ironically, her self-imposed exile from the bright lights (or at least all-night stoplights) and big (or at least medium-sized) city was brought about by the success of her first book, *Lily: A Love Story.* Published in 1992 by the prestigious Algonquin Books of Chapel Hill, North Carolina, *Lily* was a Book Club selection and was reprinted three times. With the book's success came an avalanche of requests for speeches and signings. At the time, Cindy was living in Corpus Christi, and she jokes that she probably talked to every civic group within local calling distance. In fact, it was the ever-summoning telephone that was the final straw that drew the line in the dirt (or something like that) and propelled the relocation. Yorktown ultimately was chosen for its peacefulness and solitude and small-town friendliness. "Most of all," Cindy adds, "I like Yorktown because there are fewer distractions, which allows me to really concentrate on my writing." It must be working: she won first place in the 1997 PEN Texas Award for an excerpt from her novel, *Too Close to Heaven.*

Like the characters in her novels, Cindy has contradictions in her personality that make her interesting. For instance, all authors— whether they admit it or not—seek the recognition of a critically acclaimed book. (Otherwise, they would confine their writing to journals.) But, in Cindy's case, this recognition became so burdensome that she left town. Also, not surprisingly, Cindy is happiest when she is writing, and yet, sometimes she must force herself to do the thing she most enjoys. She claims she will do anything—work the *TV Guide* crossword puzzle, dust the bottom of the dining room chairs, reorganize her husband's tool box—in order to postpone sitting down in front of an empty computer screen. If I were able to explore and then resolve these apparent incongruities in her actions, I might have the basis for a fascinating character in the novel I plan to write—that is, after I'm through dusting the refrigerator coils.

Cindy Bonner's
BOHEMIAN KOLACHES

My paternal grandmother was a Bohemian woman. She called herself this and didn't feel it was a slur, as some Czech people apparently did. The country of Czechoslovakia didn't exist when she was born in 1889 in Dime Box, Texas. Czechoslovakia came into being after World War I.

My granny's people were dirt farmers, peasant stock. They were a clannish bunch and proud of their heritage, frugal and independent. Mostly, they settled in the Blackland Prairie regions in Central and South Texas. They were hard working, but they also knew how to play hard when the right time came. Granny loved to dance. Her family sometimes traveled overnight by wagon to attend a good dance or a wedding in a distant county. And there was always good food in abundance at these gatherings—sausages, potatoes, dumplings, stuffed cabbages, and, if the occasion was special enough, kolaches.

Sadly, Granny died in 1954 when I was only a baby, so I never really knew her, but she has influenced me anyway. I have lots of pictures to inspire me, letters, newspaper clippings, and diary entries that she left behind. She didn't learn English until she was twelve, and at twenty-one she married a Texas-born man of German descent. This kind of out-marrying was frowned upon in both families, and so the couple eloped to La Grange. I have a photograph of them on their wedding day: a tiny, pretty, blond-haired Victorian lady with a big bouquet of carnations and ferns drooping in her hands; and a stiff-shouldered, proud man in a suit and tie, hair knife-parted to one side, left arm tucked militarily behind his back. In their faces I can see me and my brother, and my sons and cousins; and I can see a pioneer spirit that still lives in those of us who call ourselves Texans.

The Main Recipe
This is a recipe with yeast. Yes, yeast. But that doesn't mean it's hard. The main thing with a yeast recipe is to buy fresh yeast (check the

expiration date), and when you dissolve the yeast in warm water, make sure the water is between 105 and 115 degrees. Do those two things — use fresh yeast, and measure the temperature of your water — and any yeast recipe you try will come out just fine. It also helps to have dough hooks on your mixer.

You will need to use a large mixing bowl — the largest in your kitchen. This recipe makes four dozen kolaches.

3 packages of active dry yeast
$\frac{3}{4}$ cup of warm water (105 to 115 degrees)
$2\frac{1}{4}$ cups lukewarm milk
$\frac{3}{4}$ cup sugar
3 beaten egg yolks
$\frac{1}{4}$ cup margarine at room temperature
$\frac{1}{2}$ cup shortening
Between 9 and 10 cups all-purpose flour

Dissolve the yeast in the warm water. Add the milk. Make sure the milk is lukewarm, so it doesn't cool down the dissolved yeast. You want the yeast to stay warm. Add sugar, egg yolks, margarine, and shortening, beating after each addition. Add the flour, one cup at a time, beating until moistened. If you have dough hooks for your mixer, change over to them after about five (5) cups. Continue adding the flour one cup at a time, until the dough is well blended and begins to pull away cleanly from the sides of the bowl. The dough should be pillowy soft, but not sticky.

Sprinkle flour on your counter top or on a kneading board, and flour your hands as well. Gently lift out the dough and place it on the floured board or counter top. Knead about five times, just enough to get out any air pockets. *Do not over-knead. This makes kolaches tough.* Clean out the residue of dough from the large bowl, and dry it thoroughly. Spray with cooking oil, and return the kneaded dough to the bowl. Cover with a dry dishtowel, and set in a warm place. For this part, I turn my oven on the "warm" setting, leave the door open, and set the bowl of dough on the center of the door. Let the dough rise until it is double in size. This will take about two hours, so read a book or something.

When the dough has risen to double, scoop out golf-ball-size hunks with a medium spoon. Shape between your hands into nice, even, round balls. Place the balls two inches apart on a greased cookie sheet. You will need about four cookie sheets for this. Brush each dough ball with melted butter. Let the balls rise to double once again. Go back to reading the book you started for about another hour.

After the dough balls are double in size, press an indention in the center of each one. Do this with your fingertips. Fill each indention with a prepared fruit or cheese filling. (Don't worry, I'm going to give you a couple.) Sprinkle each kolache with a tablespoon of *posipka* (see below), and let rise again for 20 to 30 minutes. This third rising is the one that will make your kolaches melt-in-your-mouth tender.

Bake in a 400 degree oven for 15 to 20 minutes. Don't overcook. Kolaches should still be soft when taken from the oven. Brush again with butter, or use butter spray. Cool on a rack.

Posipka (Bohemian Streusel)

1 cup sugar
$1\frac{1}{4}$ cups flour
$\frac{1}{4}$ cup melted butter

In a medium bowl, blend all ingredients together with a fork. Ingredients should be the consistency of coarse-ground meal.

Cheese Filling

1 12-ounce container of cottage cheese
2 large eggs
$\frac{1}{2}$ cup butter (softened)
$\frac{3}{4}$ cup sugar

Drain cottage cheese in a strainer. Beat the eggs together. Put all the ingredients into a medium bowl and stir well. Use approximately one heaping tablespoon of filling for each kolache.

Apricot Filling

1 12-ounce package of dried apricots
$\frac{3}{4}$ cup of sugar, or additional sugar to taste

Slice apricots into pieces. Put into cooking pot. Cover the dried fruit with water and bring to a boil. Continue cooking for about 15 minutes, or until apricots are tender. Add sugar and cook until sugar is dissolved. Use approximately one heaping tablespoon of filling inside each kolache.

Note: You also can use canned pie filling if you're feeling lazy, but I warn you, it isn't the same as cooked dried fruit.

BOOKS

Lily. Chapel Hill, N.C.: Algonquin Books, 1992.
Looking after Lily. Chapel Hill, N.C.: Algonquin Books, 1994.
The Passion of Dellie O'Barr. Chapel Hill, N.C.: Algonquin Books, 1996.

Jay Brandon lives in San Antonio
where he divides his time between writing
fiction and practicing family law. He is the
author of thrillingly realistic courtroom
dramas set in Texas.

Jay Brandon

Jay Brandon's background as a trial attorney gives veracity to his legal thrillers; however, it was not the intricate plot and surprise ending of *Local Rules* that I found most compelling, but rather the love story.

I've heard it said that men don't write love scenes that women like. If that is indeed the case, Jay must have had help from his wife with one of the love scenes in the book—I have reread that part so often that my copy falls open to the page. (Oh, man!) I've been reluctant to ask Jay how he—a lawyer turned author—managed to write such a window-fogger, because I was afraid it might unfairly incriminate the lawyer I've been married to for over twenty years.

And another thing. When John Grisham and Jay Brandon are likened, it is Jay Brandon and not John Grisham who sets the curve.

Jay Brandon's
VEGETABLE TEMPLATE

A mystery writer friend of mine who writes under the name M. D. Lake advised me, "What you and I need is a template. You know what a template is, don't you?"

Of course. That paper pattern through which I drilled screws so that my under-the-counter coffee maker would be properly aligned.

"Right," M. D. went on. "A pattern. All the best-selling mystery writers use them." He mentioned a particularly well-selling mystery writer whose name I probably shouldn't disclose in this context. Not even her initials. "All her books are exactly the same," M. D. said. "She just changes the character names and a few details of setting, and uses the same plot over and over and over." And readers seem to love that, we agreed.

I thought of other great mystery writers of the past. Earl Stanley Garner. Rex Stout. Masters of the template:

"Yes, yes, I did it! I couldn't stand his sarcasm any more."

"Thank you all for coming this evening. No, no, Miss Deville. Don't sit in one of the yellow chairs. Take the red leather one."

The trouble was, I just couldn't take M. D. up on his excellent advice. At the time he gave it to me, I had just written my favorite of my novels. It was called *Local Rules,* and I loved writing it more than anything I've ever done. It wasn't like making up a story, it was like remembering. Late in the book, one character said to another, "Your hand is shaking." And I noticed that *my* hand was shaking. I was so inside the story I was living it.

I realized that I had found my template. Big-city lawyer gets caught up in small-town mystery. In a bizarro-world, everything-different way, I did it again in my next novel, *Defiance County.* And I hated every minute of it. Writing the book was just a chore. I had done it already, you see. Not precisely, not even close, really, but close enough that I took no enjoyment at all in the writing. Ironically enough, and proving M. D.'s theory, readers loved *Defiance County.* I was the only one who had too low a threshold of boredom to enjoy doing the same thing over again.

For this reason, bestsellerdom probably is forever denied me. But writing is my first, best ambition, the only thing I've wanted to do since I was ten years old. I can't let it turn into drudgery just because I've finally stumbled across my template.

I do, however, have a template for vegetables.

I don't use up any creativity on cooking. I've found one method of cooking vegetables I like, and I use it again and again. It works with either fresh or frozen vegetables, peas or broccoli or green beans. I simmer them for just a few minutes in just a little water with salt, pepper, and the herb favorite of the moment, generally basil. Then—this is the important part—I drain them and add a pat of butter and a pat of margarine (a cholesterol compromise).

When I started cooking I emulated my mother and put the butter into the boiling water, but gradually I decided on my own that the butter cooked away or got lost in the broth. My way, once you deprive the vegetable of its simmering water, it's ready to soak up every bit of the butter and margarine replacement.

No one's complained about the lack of variation in my vegetable preparation (and I have three children who complain about nearly everything else involving food). It worked once, it works forever, and the consumers are satisfied. B is for Broccoli.

The only other cooking trick I've figured out on my own is how to grill the perfect steak. For years I spent all my energy getting the coals to just the right glow and timing the steaks on the grill perfectly. ("Quick! To the table! Take a bite now! Now, it's perfect NOW! Too late.") Nonetheless, no matter how refined my method, the results were variable.

Then I discovered marinade. This helped; but my greatest discovery, as so many of them are, was by accident. I had marinated the ribeyes that afternoon as usual, but events intervened and dinner was had elsewhere. We didn't get around to the steaks until the next night. The fire was okay, I watched the clock only indifferently, I slapped the steaks on the plates.

Perfect!

Marinating was only half the secret. Time was the other ingredient. What makes the perfect grilled steak is marinating it *overnight*. It takes some forethought, but the result is always predictably great. I use a little Worcestershire sauce, a little soy sauce, some red wine, but I don't think the marinade itself is as important as duration: the patient has to soak overnight.

I could complete the circle now by returning to analogy. Marinating and, for example, atmosphere in fiction almost cry out for comparison. But I just can't bring myself to do it. Been there, you see. Done it.

Move on.

BOOKS

Deadbolt. New York: Pocket Books, 1985.
Tripwire. New York: Pocket Books, 1987.
Predator's Waltz. New York: St. Martin's, 1989.
Fade the Heat. New York: Pocket Books, 1990.
Rules of Evidence. New York: Pocket Books, 1992.
Loose Among the Lambs. New York: Pocket Books, 1993.
Local Rules. New York: Pocket Books, 1995.
Defiance County. New York: Pocket Books, 1996.
Law and Liberty: A History of the Legal Profession in San Antonio. San Antonio, Tex.: Taylor Publishing, 1996.

Rosellen Brown

Rosellen Brown currently lives in Chicago but until 1996 taught writing at the University of Houston. She is considered one of our country's best novelists. Two of her novels have been made into major motion pictures.

Rosellen Brown

The best ending I've ever read is at the end (never overlook the obvious) of *Before and After.* If you've read the book or seen the movie, you know that the plot pivots on a tragedy that ambushes a family. The story is about how the family members pick their way through the shards, dazed and disoriented, and try to right themselves in the tragedy's aftermath. The ending isn't cheerful or tied with a bow, but it is as seamless and clear as a crystal ball, telling the truth. It is the type of ending that makes you want to leave a space on the shelf beside the book. That way there is room for the imaginary pages of the balance of the characters' lives.

I know. I know. I don't have the credentials to judge what is and isn't fine writing. The last time I took an English class was in 1971, and I was barely able to eke out a B. Still, though, my unschooled opinion is that an author can spoil an otherwise outstanding book by mangling (or even slightly mishandling) the ending. Bad endings leave you feeling cheated and resentful toward the author, as if he or she is purposefully withholding something. This is never the case with Ms. Brown. When you finish one of her books, you are humbled by her generosity.

Rosellen Brown's

IN-A-HURRY TORTE

This is my prize best recipe for the All-Purpose In-a-Hurry Torte, which I ought to keep a secret because it's bailed me out in so many times of need, looking more complicated than it is, but which for that very reason I feel I ought to share.

Once when I was speaking with the extraordinary writer Tillie Olsen, I disdained some kitchen appliance—I think it may have been a dishwasher—and Tillie, who's spent a busy life not only writing but organizing labor, inspiring women (and men) everywhere, reviving interest in the great lost women writers of the past—a life with no time to waste—said to me, "Rosellen, never look an appliance in the eye. They're there to help you get on with more important things." Well, recipes like this are like those trusty kitchen helpers: You don't always have time for that fancy two-hour concoction, that Platonic ideal of a dark chocolate ganache cake, raspberries between the layers. At those times, here's what you can toss in a bowl and decorate to your heart's content. If it takes you more than five minutes, you're dawdling.

$\frac{1}{2}$ cup shortening (margarine or Crisco)
scant 1 cup sugar
2 eggs
1 cup flour
1 tsp. baking powder
Any kind of fruit, fresh (sugar-and-cinnamoned or not, to taste)
    or canned; or chocolate sauce; or nuts and cinnamon

Cream shortening and sugar, add eggs and beat. For a fluffier cake, you can separate the eggs and fold in stiffened whites later, but this really is supposed to be pretty flat (thus foolproof; you don't have to worry about rising and falling).

Combine remaining dry ingredients, add to wet. Beat for as long as you want to. Longer is better; but it's still, I repeat, not meant to be a high cake.

Topping can be used on top, but after years of doing it that way,

I've begun to put it in the middle and cover with the second half of the batter. Fruit stays more moist that way. It's up to you. If you're using chocolate sauce, that's probably better dripped on top. If you'd like, you can cut it in to make a marble cake.

Bake for about an hour at 350 degrees. Keep an eye on it; don't let it dry out.

This is not a dramatic cake, but you needn't apologize for it. In apple or bruised-peach season, when you can pile on the juicy fruit, it's especially good.

BOOKS

Street Games. Garden City, N.Y.: Doubleday, 1974.
The Autobiography of My Mother. Garden City, N.Y.: Doubleday, 1976.
Tender Mercies. New York: Knopf, 1978.
Civil Wars. New York: Knopf/Dell, 1984.
Before and After. New York: Farrar, Straus and Giroux/Dell, 1992.

POETRY

Cora Fry's Pillow Book. New York: Farrar, Straus and Giroux, 1994.

*Anita Richmond Bunkley's first novel
was published in 1989. She is best known
for her narration of the lives of
African-American families.*

Anita Richmond Bunkley

In 1989, Anita Richmond Bunkley self-published one thousand copies of her book, *Emily, The Yellow Rose*. With a friend's help, she was able to place a few copies in a well-known upscale bookstore in Houston. By mentioning this bookstore, she then was able to convince other bookstore managers that her book should be carried in their stores as well. So it was, trunkload after trunkload, that she sold her books. Ten thousand books and countless readings in public schools later, she signed a contract with Dutton to publish an adult historical novel about African-Americans, *Black Gold*. (New York publishing houses, bless their hearts, know that an author's personality and crowd appeal impact—their transitive verb, not mine—book sales. It also helps if the author writes well and taps into a largely ignored source for her stories.)

Although Anita is a successful writer, when she steps up to the microphone, it becomes clear that she has missed her calling: She needs to run for public office. First, her background as a schoolteacher gives her poise and clarity in front of an audience. Second, her graceful enthusiasm for her subject (as opposed to a talk-show brand of perkiness) is infectious. Last, she conveys subtle wonderment and gratitude that she has been asked to speak to those gathered. That quality alone would make her immensely likable. All that, before she smiles and shows her dimples.

Anita Richmond Bunkley's

CHRISTMAS CAKE

I am not much of a baker, and I don't have much of a sweet tooth, but before you groan with envy, you should know that my weakness is anything battered and deep fried. Really. Vegetables, fruit, cheese, etc. If it can be fried until it turns brown and crispy, I'll probably love it. You get the picture. However, when Christmas rolls around, I begin to feel guilty if I am not planning on baking anything. When my daughters were young, we used to make dozens of traditional butter cookies and spend hours decorating them. As they grew up, I began trying to ease out of the holiday baking, and now that my girls have their own kitchens, along with the recipes and the cookie cutters I used as a child, I can finally look forward to them ringing my doorbell with plastic-covered trays of Santas, angels, and elves, all crusted over with sprinkles and sugar.

About fifteen years ago, a coworker gave me a recipe that solved my dilemma of baking something special for the holidays. The first time I tasted this dessert, I immediately fell in love with it. The cake wows my dinner guests and has everyone believing that I really do get elbow deep in flour and eggs on a regular basis. This cake is suited for experimentation, although I've never tried any of the variations I'll suggest here. I guess I really don't want to mess with what has been the traditional cake that I love to make for family and friends during the holidays.

You need a rectangular glass baking dish, like a Pyrex lasagna pan, approximately 8 x 18 inches. Using a glass dish is a nice idea, because you'll serve the cake directly from this pan and everyone can see the colorful layers. But if you only have a metal pan, I'm sure it would work just fine.

You will need:

1 box white cake mix
1 large-size box strawberry Jell-O
1 large Jell-O vanilla instant pudding
2 pkgs. Dream Whip

Buy a pretty good quality BOX white cake mix. Prepare the BOX cake as directed. (I've never made a white cake from scratch, but if that's your thing, go for it.) When you pour the cake into the pan, it will look as if there is too much batter for the pan, but there isn't. It will all level out. Bake as directed, and let it cool completely. This can be done the day before.

Make the strawberry Jell-O as directed—but use ONE-HALF the water called for. This is very important!! (You can use lime Jell-O if you'd like a St. Patrick's Day cake, orange if you'd like a Halloween cake, etc. These variations sound great, but as I said, I've never strayed from the Original Recipe.) Let the Jell-O cool, but don't let it begin to set up.

Using a toothpick, punch holes all over the white cake.

Pour the cooled Jell-O over the cake. Fix the pudding per directions. (Again, you could vary the flavor of pudding according to your taste and the holiday.) Spread the pudding over the cake.

Whip 2 packages of Dream Whip. I've even used Cool Whip in a pinch. I suppose you could add a drop of food coloring to the Dream Whip . . . get the idea? Carefully spread the whipped topping over the pudding.

Put the cake in the refrigerator to chill completely before serving.

Right before presentation, I garnish the top of my fluffy white cake with *well drained* maraschino cherries and sprigs of mint arranged like a big wreath. If the cherries are wet, the red juice will stain the whipped topping, so be sure to dry them off. If you are making the cake for a different holiday, you can be very creative with your garnishes. Cut the cake into squares to serve.

That's it. A pretty cake that everyone loves, and it takes very little time. Maybe this year, I'll be brave enough to try out some of my suggested variations and give everyone a big surprise!

BOOKS

Emily, the Yellow Rose. Houston: Rinard, 1989.
Black Gold. New York: Dutton, 1994.
Wild Embers. New York: Dutton, 1995.
Starlight Passage. New York: Dutton, 1996.

Norma E. Cantú

*Norma Elia Cantú is professor of English
at Texas A&M International University
in Laredo, her hometown.*
Canícula: Snapshots of a Girlhood en la
Frontera *is her first book.*

Norma Elia Cantú

When I was fifteen years old, I announced to my family that I had decided to be an English teacher. Somewhat surprised, my father replied, "Deborah, you're not smart enough to be a teacher. Besides, what would you do with an English degree? You need to go to medical school." I received a medical degree when I was twenty-five, which was fairly unremarkable, given the circumstances.

One hundred and fifty miles to the south, another conversation took place between another Texas girl and her father. After scholastic aptitude tests proved intellectual superiority in language skills and science, Norma Elia Cantú announced to her family that she had decided to study science, perhaps chemistry or physics. Her father reacted with a bemused smile and said in his most formal, gentle Spanish, "Women do not study science. Besides, why do you want to go to college? A smart girl like you can get a job with good benefits."

Because he had supported her earlier dreams of becoming a teacher, she understands in retrospect, that her father's misgivings about her studying science stemmed from the family's brittle financial situation and not from any intention to discourage her. After high school graduation, she attended Laredo Junior College on a scholarship, but after the first year, when the scholarship money ran out, she did get that job with good benefits, at Central Power and Light Company. She continued attending night school until Texas A&I opened a branch in Laredo and she was able to finish her bachelor's degree. Despite unpaved roads and washed-out bridges along the way, Norma Elia Cantú received her Ph.D. in English from the University of Nebraska in Lincoln in 1982. She was thirty-five years old, which was nothing short of remarkable, given the circumstances.

As Dr. Cantú writes about her years growing up in Laredo's economically strapped, ninety-percent-Latino community, there is only one place in her narrative where I sense blistering anger: "The politicos. Our money lines their pockets, paves private roads on their ranches, while our streets remain unpaved, run like rivers after every rain, while our public library remains as small as someone's private library; while the dropout rate remains between 50 and 80 percent; while judges, mayors, sheriffs, high and low powerful ones abuse, rape, embarrass, harass, taunt, demean women."

In 1980, Dr. Cantú chose to return to her hometown and is now professor of English at Texas A&M International University. She also is a major player in the city's tardy but successful effort to create a top-shelf public library. In addition, she writes and works with a women's group, Las Mujeres, and a number of community-based organizations, including the Literacy Volunteers of America—Laredo, which she founded in 1985. I didn't think to ask her if she plans to run for public office. Such a decision would be fairly unremarkable, given her indomitability—in spite of, and quite possibly because of, her circumstances.

Norma Elia Cantú's

CAPIROTADA: A LENTEN TREAT

When I was growing up, I awaited Lent eagerly every year, although often it meant going without chewing gum or my favorite candy, Cracker Jacks. And, if I wanted to really suffer, as I imagined I had to, to atone for sins real or potential, the ultimate sacrifice was to deny myself movies. The denial lasted all forty days of Lent. But without fail, every Friday of Lent, along with the sacrifices came the treat— capirotada.

A typical Lenten meal would consist of fish soup; nopalitos, the tender pencas of the prickly pear in our backyard, cooked in Mami's special sauce; and sopa de arroz cooked with tiny dried shrimp. This "sopa," in the typical northern Mexico/South Texas style, is not a soup but a rice dish. The fish soup, on the other hand, is a more traditional liquidy soup. The entree would consist of fish, lightly breaded and fried, and albóndigas de salmon, tuna fish, or, my favorite, powdered shrimp. In most of Mexico and Spain, *albóndigas* refers to meatballs, but in South Texas and northern Mexico the word refers to the batter-dipped and fried croquettes typically prepared during Lent. Mami sometimes varies the menu by substituting the fish or the albóndigas with Enchiladas Mejicanas, made with corn tortillas dipped in a red chile sauce before lightly frying and filled with white cheese and onions, unlike the American ones filled with cheddar cheese and smothered with chile con carne.

In spite of all these delicacies, I cared for but one thing: the bread pudding that one of my younger sisters rejected because of its (to her) unappetizing name, capirotada. Once the rest of us enticed her to taste it, though, she became a fellow addict. Before eating it, however, she still removes the raisins and the cheese, exactly what some of us like best. Mami still makes capirotada; but now that the household has been reduced from eleven children to only one still living with them, my parents often eschew cooking the traditional meals. But, at least on Lenten Fridays, they prepare special meals, and invariably there's enough capirotada left over so that many a grandchild will come by after school for the inimitable treat.

In Laredo I don't make capirotada; after all, my mother makes it, and much better than mine. While living in Madrid and later in Washington, D.C., though, I have made capirotada—substituting brown sugar for the piloncillos so readily available in any grocery store in Laredo, and paying an arm and a leg for a few pecan pieces. But it's never the same. It could be the substitution, but I think it's my mother's touch that makes all the difference.

I hope you enjoy this delicious treat. By the way, you don't have to wait for Lent, nor do you have to give up any goodies, to enjoy it; but somehow all the suffering and small deprivations during Lent make it all that more delicious.

First, a warning: as in almost all traditional foods, the measurements I am listing here are mere approximations. You have to try the recipe a couple of times to know exactly what works for you. My mother, who doesn't even own a measuring cup or measuring spoon, agreed to these measurements a few years ago when I videotaped her and my sisters as we prepared a typical Lenten Friday meal.

6 cups of water
1 medium-size package of cinnamon sticks
1 small package of anise seed
3 large piloncillos of raw sugar (each can be substituted with a
    cup of dark brown sugar)
2 loaves day-old French bread
1½ pound mild cheddar cheese
1 cup raisins
1 cup pecan pieces

Bring water to boil, add cinnamon and anise. (The sizes of the packages cited are from the standard "La India Packing Company" in Laredo.) Add piloncillos or brown sugar and stir until all sugar is dissolved. The piloncillo is raw sugar as it is made in the moliendas and usually comes in various sizes. A small piloncillo mashed up will fill a standard cup. For this recipe use the medium ones—that is, about a cup and a half. The mixture is called melcocha; some people call it "miel de piloncillo."

Butter sides and bottom of a 2-quart pot.

Slice day-old French bread. If you didn't have the foresight to get the bread the day before making the capirotada, you can place the slices on a cookie sheet and lightly toast it in the oven. Layer slices in the pot, with slices of cheese, raisins, and pecan pieces. We usually use pecans from the tree in our neighbor's yard, but you can buy packages of Texas pecans pretty much anywhere. You also can try layering other things, as they do along the Arizona border, where they use apples and bananas as well. When the pot is relatively full, pour boiling hot melcocha/miel over the entire concoction.

Cover and let sit for 10 minutes.

Serves 12 or so, depending on hunger. Although it is a typical dessert for Lenten meals and usually is eaten warm, some folks prefer leftover capirotada as an evening snack and swear that it is even better cold. Some of my siblings eat it *a la mode* with a scoop of vanilla ice cream. When we were kids, Mami often would double the recipe. Nowadays she halves it.

BOOKS

Canícula: Snapshots of a Girlhood en la Frontera. Albuquerque: University of New Mexico Press, 1995.

*Liz Carpenter began as a journalist and has
published both fiction and non-fiction.
She has also held numerous political
appointments including Press Secretary
to Lady Bird Johnson.*

Liz Carpenter

I've found that truly funny people are funniest when they depart from their prepared remarks and wander over into the margins. So it was with Liz Carpenter when she spoke at the First Annual Texas Book Festival in Austin. Playing to a packed house (or more accurately, a packed hearing room) at the Capitol, she charmed us with humorous anecdotes about being press secretary for Lady Bird Johnson, being a profoundly busy working mother while rearing her own two children, and the life-widening experiences and dratted inconveniences of being a septuagenarian: "I'm down to one of everything. One good ear. One good eye. One good leg. And one bosom, although I don't think having two of them would have done me much good."

She also read a passage from *Unplanned Parenthood,* a funny and poignant book about finding herself, at age seventy, the surrogate mother to her deceased brother's three teen-aged children. Believing that life is bearable if one has a sense of purpose and a sense of humor, she rose mightily to the challenge. When asked if she would again accept the often thankless task, she answered thoughtfully, "I'd rather do it than not do it or fail to do it. Yes, I'm glad I did it—there wasn't any other chance for them. Besides, there's nothing more aging than not to be needed."

I want it written down somewhere that Liz Carpenter is my hero.

Liz Carpenter
ET TU, LITTLE CAESAR'S?

(An excerpt from the book *Unplanned Parenthood,* describing the dilemmas involved in providing food for teenagers. Used with permission of Random House.)

Three hungry appetites send me to the grocery store almost daily. I think I spend more time there than the manager.

Tommy says he'll gladly take over the task when he can drive, and I am getting as eager as he is for this to happen. Sixteen is the legal driving age in Texas, but you can get a hardship license at fifteen if you can prove your family has a hardship. I think I have lots of them, but my bad ankle and advancing age are all we'll need to qualify Tommy for the special license. I'm counting down the minutes.

Meanwhile, I am becoming less picky about old-fashioned nutritious meals.

Kids are omnivorous, but they like it plain. So, forget the caviar. Put away the oyster forks. Throw out the Charlotte russe pan. These kids will eat anything. They can go through a bowl of grapes faster than César Chávez could have picked them. At this house, we don't know what leftovers are!

When school is out, danger! I used to think of this hour as "snack time." Those words are too gentle. If the breakfast counter doesn't have anything edible on it, they will eat the breakfast counter. Raging hunger is a common trait.

And beware if dinner is cooked and waiting on the stove. More than once I have thrown my body in front of it in a spread-eagle position to save it for later. One Easter Sunday I had prepared dinner for friends who were coming back from church service with me. I came home with them to find the roast cleaned to the bone. Tommy had eaten it all for breakfast.

Why is it this comes as a shock to me? Because when I was raising my own two teenagers, I had a cook, a marvelous North Carolina woman named Ruth. Where is Ruth now that I really need her? Well, she's working at a bank where "I have my own desk," she told me proudly when I called her long distance. So the cooking for these three hungry teenagers falls on me, and it is five times more than the grocery bill for one widow.

Today's hunger rush prompts me to remember long ago on a safari to Africa that I watched the mother lions kill a wildebeest, leave it a few moments, so the male lions can come in for the best parts, and when the Kings of the Jungle had done their damage, the docile lionesses returned for the bones. Here at my home on Skyline Drive, the "Kings of the Jungle" are Tommy and his friends—all 14- to 16-year-old males. You can almost hear them roar, "FOOD!" at the ice box door.

I don't mean to make light of the problems of Bosnia, but the United Nations should know that I could use an airlift of edibles, too.

I've always loved to cook, but my repertoire had really shrunk over the years. I'd forgotten how hard it is to come up with something different for dinner night after night. Liz, Tommy, and Mary weren't exactly picky eaters—Lord knows these are kids who'd eat meatloaf for breakfast and think Chef Boyardee really owns a restaurant somewhere—but I felt obliged to try to vary what I put on the table. How many nights in a row can Perdue *do* it? Plus I was going broke buying prepared foods and Chinese take-out. Something had to give.

So I consulted the nearest food experts, my sister-in-law Jean, who is a home economics professor, and a good friend, Anita Davis, who is the Julia Child of Westlake Hills. Anita can be seen on most any special day—Ash Wednesday, Shrove Tuesday, Groundhog Day—bearing cakes and cookies to some class at school.

Anita was ready. A picturesque smorgasbord lay before us. This table didn't just groan. It screamed.

Pigs in blankets, carrot sticks and three kinds of dips, Anita's Super Lasagna oozing with hot melted cheese, a big platter of chicken rolled and baked with a crushed cornflake crust, a plate of pita pockets, and a baked potato bar with all the fixin's—butter, sour cream, bacon bits, and cheese toppings. These potatoes were grown for mature sizes only.

All this was just for starters. The smorgasbord lopped over onto the sideboard for desserts. There was a giant plate of pancake-size cookies with smiling faces on them in raisins and red hots, then an assorted plate of three of her best cookie recipes: a hand-sized sugar cookie shaped like a map of Texas with raisins marking the major cities, chewy brownies, and—yes—the family favorite, chocolate chip cookies. She informed us there was plenty of ice cream in assorted flavors in the freezer if anyone wanted it. The evening had grown from a taste test to a feast. But what the hey? It all worked great, and the kids' eyes grew wide when they saw the spread. Forget about the way to a man's heart. Food is for getting to teenagers.

The kids were like race horses straining at the gate as I said a hurried blessing: "Thank you, God, for a bounty that only You and Anita could cook up."

And then we were into it! For twenty-five minutes conversation was at a standstill. The only sound was munching and crunching. The piles of food began to disappear. Anita had set up the array to be eaten chronologically—snacks, entrees, and desserts—but order was a victim of the stampede.

Mary was already trying to stretch one giant bite of Texas cookie from Corpus Christi to Amarillo into her mouth, and Tommy and friends were inhaling the chicken and lasagna.

Finally, though, they were full. Anita smiled in happy satisfaction and handed out plastic baggies to take home.

But not before we polled the group for favorites. And the winners? The do-it-yourself potato bar was first by a landslide. Anita's Super Lasagna came in second, and George Bush's Broccoli, third. (What do you expect from a Republican?)

First-Prize Potato Bar

Select two large potatoes for each guest (one apiece if the guests aren't teens).

Scrub clean, grease, and make holes with fork.

Bake in 350 degree oven for one full hour or until a fork slides in easily.

Slice each potato open four ways and arrange on platter.

Put bowls of sour cream, bacon bits, butter, chives, salt and pepper to taste.

Place all these on a counter or bar. Let them have at it.

Second-Prize Super Lasagna

1 box (8 oz.) lasagna noodles
$\frac{3}{4}$ lb. ground beef
$\frac{3}{4}$ lb. medium hot sausage meat
1 jar (30 oz.) spaghetti sauce

2 eggs
1 carton (16 oz.) cottage cheese
16 oz. mozzarella cheese, shredded
2 tbs. minced parsley, fresh or dried

Cook lasagna noodles. After draining the noodles, cover with cold water to keep them from sticking together. Meanwhile, crumble and brown the ground beef and sausage, stirring and separating with a fork. Drain off fat. Add sauce, stir, and set aside.

In a separate bowl, mix eggs, cottage cheese, mozzarella (saving $\frac{1}{2}$ cup for topping), and parsley.

Coat the bottom of a 12 x 8 inch baking dish with sauce mixture. Layer lasagna noodles, $\frac{1}{3}$ of the sauce, and $\frac{1}{2}$ of the cheese mixture. Repeat. Top with noodles, the remainder of the sauce, and the $\frac{1}{2}$ cup of mozzarella.

Bake in a 350 degree oven for one hour. Let sit for 10–15 minutes before cutting in squares and serving.

If there are leftovers, wrap individually in plastic wrap, freeze, and pop in the microwave for single servings.

Third-Prize Broccoli Fit for George Bush
(Who Never Liked the Stuff)

Steam fresh or frozen broccoli parts. Make white sauce with sherry and add almond slivers. Or you can mix Dijon mustard and plain yogurt for a tasty, healthful alternative.

My contribution to the testing and tasting party were educational fortune cookies. Mary and Liz both love Chinese food and think the fortune cookies should guide them through life. I came up with a way to convey my messages and not be accused of preaching. I bought fortune cookies and with tweezers slipped out the store-bought fortune and inserted one of my own with tiny hand-printed messages. This requires patience and a Machiavellian mind. Here are some of my favorites:

He who wears dirty T-shirt must use Chinese laundry.
Homework begun gets done.
He who speeds pays for costly deeds.

Periods of household improvement are in your future.
Too little work causes Looney Teens.
He who washes plate will be rewarded.

The possibilities are endless, particularly if you do this after downing two glasses of champagne. Once this prompted me to write:

Sex gives acne!
Too much hard rock leads to early deafness.

Tommy added one other:

Confucius say: "He who lies with the women forget not his condom-ents."

BOOKS

Ruffles and Flourishes. Garden City, N.Y.: Doubleday, 1969.
Getting Better All the Time. New York: Simon & Schuster, 1987.
Unplanned Parenthood. New York: Random House, 1994.

Jim W. Corder is the author of numerous
textbooks and articles on rhetoric, as well as
creative non-fiction about his native West
Texas. He is professor of English at Texas
Christian University.

Jim W. Corder

A drill in beginner essay writing classes is to list the things you know about or feel strongly about. This way you can pinpoint subjects that you might want to explore in your writing. Coming from another angle, recurring ideas in journal entries might indicate potential topics for an article or book. So that we won't discount our lists as trivial, writing teachers reassure us that if we think something is significant, surely someone else will, too. (Maybe not an acquisitions editor, but surely someone.)

Dr. Jim Corder claims—not meaning it as a joke, really, because he is a contemplative and subdued, some might even say melancholic, man—that he has only one book to write. He just keeps writing it over and over. Of course, that's not true. What is true, though, is that strong themes pulsate through all of his non-scholastic writing. (Besides the listed titles, he also has written textbooks about the principles of rhetoric, in the full sense of that word.)

A recurring theme is looking for something that perpetually eludes him. This inability to find something that is familiar is due to the impermanence of all things—people, places, ideas, even the written word. No matter how skillfully we delude ourselves, and no matter how frantically we strive to leave our mark, we are all fleeting glimpses, wispy bits of smoke. No, Dr. Corder's writing is not cheerful, because he turns full-face to what haunts every one of us that stops distracting ourselves long enough to pay attention. Still, though, he shows profound gentleness and kindness toward his readers by having the courage to write it down: "If we acknowledge and name the anxieties, fears, difficulties, and problems that are out there waiting for us, they don't go away, to be sure, but they're not quite so scary. It's easier to deal with the ghost behind the next tree if you have a name for it."

Jim W. Corder's
TEACAKES

I first thought that I'd tell about the dressing my mother made to go with a Thanksgiving turkey, but the recipe that my wife inherited from my mother through my sister makes enough for forty people, and I'm not that good about dividing the portions down to manageable sizes.

Then I thought that I'd tell about hominy, but that isn't much of a recipe. The only thing that would liven it up would be for me to show the different ways I've tried to disguise hominy so as to trick my wife into eating some. None of them worked.

I thought, too, about the recipe for Texas caviar, but then I reckoned that everybody already knew that.

After a while, I thought that I'd share the recipe for Croton Breaks paté, but I created that recipe myself, and I'll be damned if I'll give it away for nothing.

And I thought about telling how I learned from my wife what you can do with a whole stick of bologna when you cook it for hours in a slow oven, but that's a special treat, and I'm too selfish to scatter knowledge of it all over the earth, though you surely can have some if you come over to the house. At a Christmas party at our place one time, one of my nephews thought maybe it was a Christian baby when it came out of the oven, but he ate a plateful anyway.

Finally, I decided that I'd share the recipe for teacakes. All I can be sure about is that it makes teacakes pretty much the way my mother made them when I was a boy. It may be a common recipe for Texas Teacakes or for Southern Teacakes (my mother was a Durham, and her line came out of North Carolina by way of Georgia and Tennessee before they got to Texas), or maybe even English Teacakes.

They were my favorite food when I was a boy, but a calamity came, and teacakes disappeared from the household. My mother didn't have a recipe written down; she made them out of her head. I should tell you that she was a stubborn and prideful woman. One day when I was in the fourth grade, she made a batch. I don't know what happened, but they didn't come out to suit her, so she said, "Well, fiddle," threw them out, and vowed never to make them again. And she didn't.

By the time I was grown, I was pretty nostalgic and hungry for those teacakes. I asked my mother to tell me the recipe, but she said she didn't remember it. That may have been true, but it may be that she was still being stubborn and prideful. After a while, she died, and I couldn't ask her anymore. Meanwhile, I set out, not systematically and constantly, but pretty regularly, to reconstitute the recipe. I read recipes in magazines and newspapers and cookbooks. I made some awful cookies. I made some cookies that were pretty good but didn't have quite the right taste. One time I substituted bacon grease for the shortening, remembering that in the early years we were often pretty shy of money and that she might very well have more of the one available than the other. That produced vile cookies that I threw out in my turn. Finally, I settled on the recipe I've given, and while I can't testify that it's exactly right, it's close enough to be comforting.

4 cups of all-purpose flour
4 tsp. of baking powder
a pinch of salt
1 cup shortening (or butter or margarine)
2 cups of sugar
2 eggs
$\frac{1}{2}$ cup of milk
2 tsp. of vanilla or lemon extract

What you do is take a large mixing bowl, and in it sift together the first three ingredients. Then, when I see how big a pile that makes, I transfer it over to our biggest mixing bowl. I don't make teacakes all that often, and my memory doesn't always serve me.

Then, in another bowl, I cream the sugar and the shortening.

Then, in another bowl, I beat the eggs lightly. When that is done, I add the eggs to the shortening mixture and mix well.

By now, I have two bowls to look at, the largest of our bowls with the sifted flour, baking powder, and salt, and a smaller bowl with the sugar, shortening, and egg mixture, and I am able to see that memory has failed me again. If I combine what's in the two bowls, which I'm supposed to do, there is about to be a helluva pile of dough. I transfer the dry mixture from our largest mixing bowl into our largest pot, the one we cook pasta in. Then I can add the shortening, sugar, and egg mixture to that, together with the milk, and the vanilla, and have room enough to mix it all well.

Then I knead it lightly on a floured board, and roll it out. Those who are interested only in a nice cookie, but a mere cookie, may roll the dough out thin, and that will give them a pleasant crisp cookie. The discriminating, however, will roll the dough thick; that will give cakes that are lightly browned on the bottom, nice and thick, and soft on top. I cut them out with something large enough to make a respectable cake—I favor a Mason jar turned upside down—and then put them on a greased cookie sheet, and cook them in a 350-degree oven for twelve or thirteen minutes. It's a good idea to cool them on a rack.

When they're cool enough to touch, I eat them. For an interesting variation, you can take two freshly cooked cakes and put between them one cut but uncooked cake. This practice, however, besides using up three cakes at a time, tends toward the orgiastic and decadent, and so I do not often indulge myself. Taken either way, the single cake or the sandwich cake, they are just about the best thing I have ever eaten. I pretty much doubt that manna ever tasted better in whatever wilderness need.

Yields 8 or 9 dozen.

BOOKS

Lost in West Texas. College Station: Texas A&M University Press, 1988.
Chronicle of a Small Town. College Station: Texas A&M University Press, 1989.
Yonder, Life on the Far Side of Change. Athens: University of Georgia Press, 1992.
Hunting Lieutenant Chadbourne. Athens: University of Georgia Press, 1993.
And others

*Elizabeth Crook is well known for her
historical fiction. Her second novel,* Promised
Lands: A Novel of the Texas Rebellion *was
edited by the late Jackie Onassis.*

Elizabeth Crook

I have attended writing classes for many years. The down side is that these classes are a guilt-free way to avoid facing The Screen. The up side is that I have heard the basics over and over. One of the cardinal rules of elegant writing is to be excruciatingly precise. This means that a writer must be passionate enough about the subject to do patient and thorough research. Or, to repeat a well-worn phrase: Sweat the details.

In her historical novels, Elizabeth Crook does just that. In the afterword to *Promised Lands,* Stephen Harrigan describes—in an awe-struck tone, if I'm reading him right—the behind-the-words research for her novel about the Texas Revolution. To keep track of details, she created a gridded calendar of 217 rectangles, each representing a day between October 1835 and April 1836. In teensy-weensy handwriting, she filled the spaces with a "wealth of eccentric detail."

In the medical profession, we attach long, fancy-sounding words to things. The medical term for teensy-weensy handwriting is *micrographia.* The medical term for preoccupation with details is *obsessive-compulsive disorder.* Call it what you like. With Elizabeth Crook, the result is crisp, fine writing.

Elizabeth Crook's
SATURDAY MORNING
ANIMAL PANCAKES

These pancakes are for children. If you make them for yourself, there is something the matter with you.

The ingredients are:

Aunt Jemima Buttermilk Pancake mix
Milk
Kretschmer's Wheat Germ
Lowfat shredded mozzarella cheese (Yes, cheese.)

When I was growing up, an imaginative woman named Esperanza Valdez worked in our home. She was from Mexico and did not speak any English, but she learned a lot of phrases from listening to my brother and sister and me talk to one another, like "Shut up." From listening to my parents, she learned words like "darling." Her favorite music was Swan Lake and she used to crank it up while we made Saturday Morning Animal Pancakes. She would tell us, "Shut up, darling," if we got so loud she couldn't hear the music. Esperanza was a mystic who believed in the powers of cheese, and it was she who started putting mozzarella in our pancake batter. Mother swore we wouldn't eat it, but we did. We liked it. Mother is the one who added wheat germ; she was into yoga and French lessons and homemade, no-nitrate sack lunches instead of school cafeteria food when our period of Animal Pancakes was at its height. Wheat germ invaded every food we ate and we had to mooch off all our neighbors to get a decent meal.

Saturday Morning Animal Pancakes can be made on any morning of the week but are the most fun on Saturdays because that is when the neighborhood friends have spent the night and are still around for breakfast. The amount of batter, of course, depends on the number of friends. The amount of individual ingredients depends on how healthy you want to be; my sister, who now has three children of her own, uses just enough Aunt Jemima to bond the wheat germ with the cheese. Basically, just pour some Aunt Jemima in a bowl, dump in a handful of low-fat shredded mozzarella, sprinkle on some wheat germ—about one-fourth of a cup or more if you are cooking for four children—then pour in enough milk to mix everything into the right consistency for pancake batter. Spray some Pam or melt some butter on a hot iron skillet.

The children should line up: Animal Pancakes are a one-at-a-time operation and must be closely supervised. Have a stool or a chair ready for the children to stand on, and a big spoon. Get the skillet sizzling hot.

Most children declare beforehand that they are going to make a dog or a horse or a hippopotamus and then blob on spoonfuls of batter that meld together to resemble, of course, nothing at all. Surprisingly, these children are rarely disappointed. Others carefully deposit appropriate amounts of batter for head, body, tail, ears, even claws, creating a masterpiece, and take their pancake off to be eaten with the complaint that one paw is bigger than the other three. I myself, as a child with no artistic talent, found it easier to spoon on globs of batter and then wait to see what developed. This is still the way I create characters in prose.

When I was home last Christmas, my mother was supervising Animal Pancakes for all her grandchildren and a couple of their friends. My nephew David, who was five, made a perfect lion, then proceeded to attach a huge elongated shape to its nose. We thought the piece was ruined, until he announced with satisfaction, pointing to the appendage, "There's the lion's roar." Later, one of my nieces dumped almost the whole bowlful of batter into the center of the pan. As we watched it spread to cover the entire pan, way out to the edges, someone asked the inevitable: "What is it?" "It's a pancake animal," she said. Silly us.

Some children are less decisive and will stare at their work until it is cold on the plate, saying, "It's a bear, no it's a cat—see, that's its tail. No, it's not its tail, it's a leash. Yeah, it's a leash. So it's a dog on a leash. Or a bear on a leash. Can you put a bear on a leash?"

The more daring are happy to put their bears on leashes, infuriating those more conscientious. I once overheard an argument break out over a particularly rotund Animal Pancake, one child declaring she had made a cloud, her older sister contending that a cloud was not an animal. "Yes it is," the younger answered flippantly. "Clouds are animals all the time." How can you argue with that?

For me, eating Animal Pancakes was always more problematic than creating them, because by the age of five I had developed an unshakable belief that everything, even inanimate objects, could "feel." I spent a lot of time at the piano, not playing it but apologizing to the individual keys in extremely high or low ranges that did not get much attention. I also had a hard time peeling bananas. With an Animal Pancake, I usually would talk gently to it for a moment, then suddenly lop its head off. This way the animal had no idea what was coming and felt no pain. I also, for obvious reasons, did not allow my animals to watch the others being eaten. My older brother, however, had a child's wicked eye for human foibles and caught on to my rituals. He sometimes would torment me while he ate his own pancakes, dismembering the creatures one limb at a time and relishing each bite . . . a leg . . . an ear . . . a piece cut from the heart. This would make me wild, and there were times when Saturday Morning Animal Pancakes had to be shut down.

You may be wondering now if these pancakes are really any good. They are! Keep in mind they will be chewier than what you're used to, because of the cheese. Don't try to cook them to the fluffy texture of normal pancakes; they will never get there. The chances are that what you think is uncooked batter is really melted cheese.

BOOKS

The Raven's Bride. Garden City, N.Y.: Doubleday, 1991.
Promised Lands. Garden City, N.Y.: Doubleday, 1994.

John R. Erish [signature]

John Erickson is best known for his
Hank the Cowdog *series, but he has*
published as well a number of nonfiction books
about the American West.

John Erickson

I have never sat down and read a single *Hank the Cowdog* book. How-ever, I am well-versed in this hero's adventures because of the many, many funny passages that have been read aloud to me by my son An-drew. When we go out to supper, my husband and daughter and I frequently get Andrew to tell us about the latest Hank escapade. After we've laughed at the newest story, we might talk over some of our favorite past episodes. Like when Hank's sidekick Drover fainted at the beginning of a fight that he and Hank had picked with a pit bull. Or when Hank mistook Sinister the Bobcat for a barn cat and jumped on him. Or when Hank was bitten in the face by a rattlesnake. Or when he became convinced that a corncob was incalculably valuable.

Although Hank's adventures provide high-stepping, leg-lifting entertainment, the story of the author who created Hank the Cowdog is even more fascinating. In fact, John Erickson's life has all the plot devices necessary for a television docudrama. A small-town Texas boy with strong family values discovers love for the written word, goes off to a big university to study English and to become a writer, and is rejected by graduate schools. Discouraged, he returns home to work as a cowboy in order to support his family but continues (notice, please, that I am resisting the urge to say "with dogged determina-tion") to write his stories early in the morning. Publishers reject his stories, time after time. He reaches a low point where he thinks he might die if he can't share his stories; with his pregnant wife's bless-ing, he borrows money and self-publishes a book, which he sells in feed stores and drugstores and Western-wear stores. One of the char-acters fills a readers' niche and is developed into a book series; a big publishing house discovers his books, and he sells two million copies. Still unassuming and with strong family values intact, he continues to live in the little Texas town, writing his stories early in the morning and singing in the Methodist choir.

The *Hank the Cowdog* series is geared towards that vast, reading-resistant herd of little boys (like mine) who would prefer to be outdoors, running and playing and getting dirty. Still, if you can get them to stop long enough to read one of Erickson's books or to listen to one of his audio cassettes, they become Hank-bitten. And, as suited as the Hank stories are for little boys, they carry gentle messages that we all would do well to heed: Be compassionate. Accept responsibility for your actions. Be reliable. Have a sense of humor. Forgive mistakes in yourself and others. Use your God-given wits and talents to overcome problems. Help others with their problems. Go out bravely to meet life. Be kind. Frankly, I think Erickson's books are misshelved in the bookstores. They don't belong in the juvenile section. They belong over in adult self-help.

John Erickson's
BACHELOR COWBOY'S DELIGHT

I am now in my fifth decade of this life's adventure. Along the way, I have compiled a list of "truisms," I guess you might call them, which preserve and communicate wisdom in a compressed form.

"If it ain't broke, don't fix it."

"There's no such thing as free love."

"Figure the worth of a horse by the cost of hospital care."

"Riding broncs is for people who don't owe money."

And there's another one which applies to this project: "Any culture that denigrates the preparation of food and the raising of children isn't nearly as smart as it thinks."

My wife is an excellent cook. She puts a lot of time and thought into the preparation of food. She reads recipes, plans menus, and shops for the ingredients. Even more astounding is that she cleans up her messes.

I admire good cooks, but I'm not one myself. I don't have the patience for it. When Kris and the kids go to Dallas to visit the kinfolks, I'm left to batch at the ranch. I never go hungry, but there isn't much variety in my menu or routine. In her absence, I use one plate, one fork, one knife, one glass, and one cooking pot. I rinse them after each meal but don't exactly wash them. I've never figured out how to run the dishwasher. Our children get paid for that.

When I'm batching, I eat the same meal over and over: a lettuce salad, frozen green peas, and sirloin steak, cooked outside on the grill. Kris gets tired of eating the same meal day after day. I don't. She gets tired of eating the same meat two days in a row. Not me. I love beef. I could eat it three times a day.

Our beef isn't the beef you buy in the store. We raise it here on the ranch and butcher it right off of grass. This is called "grass-fed" or "grass-fat" beef, as opposed to beef that has been fattened on grain in a pen or a feedlot.

Grass-fat beef is very lean. It has a dark red color, very little marbling, and a thick rind of fat around the edge. It is tougher than finished beef and has a distinctive flavor which reminds me a bit of venison.

We started eating grass-fat beef when I was cowboying in Oklahoma in 1974. On most ranches, beef is part of a cowboy's wages, and it is usually an animal that comes straight off of grass. It might be an animal with some small defect (a barren heifer or a dwarfy steer), but one in good health and gaining weight.

Once I had eaten grass-fat beef, I found it difficult to go back to store-bought. Store-bought beef seemed flat and tasteless. I didn't care for the texture (too mushy, not chewy enough), and it was always too fat. The fat on a store-bought steak reminds me of lard, whereas the fat on a grass beef is good to eat. There isn't much of it. When I cook a grass-fed steak on the grill, I never have grease fires.

I butcher a beef that weights 600 to 1,000 pounds on the hoof, and I choose a time of year when the animal is gaining weight—June or July, after green grass has come, or October, just before the first Panhandle freeze drops the protein level of the grass. I haul him to a little packing house in Perryton and let them do the butchering.

I always tell them to "hang" my beef for two weeks. After they have cut the carcass into halves, they hang it in a cooler where the temperature is around 40 degrees. You hang a beef to tenderize it. At 40 degrees, bacteria will soften the muscle fibers. That may sound unappetizing to some, but it works; and the aging process also give the meat a deeper flavor, reminiscent of cheese.

In the seventies, when we lived on a ranch in Oklahoma, I used to kill my own beeves, skin them out, cut them into quarters, and take the quarters into town, where a moonlighting butcher would cut them up into steaks and roasts. I enjoyed participating in the process, but that came to an end in 1977, when the State of Oklahoma, in its wisdom, passed a law that forbade butchers from cutting up meat for individuals.

Ostensibly, this was to protect the public from something or other, but I suspect that it had more to do with protecting the jobs of union meatcutters in Oklahoma City.

So now let us turn to my recipes for Bachelor Cowboy's Delight.

Steak

1 grass-fat sirloin steak. Sprinkle both sides with garlic salt. Cook each side five minutes on a hot fire, either on an open-flame gas grill or mesquite coals. Don't overcook it.

Salad

Chop up half a head of lettuce. If you're inspired, throw in some chopped up celery, mushrooms, and punkin seeds. Dress the salad with the juice of half a lime, olive oil, soy sauce, and green Tabasco sauce.

Vegetables

Throw a handful of frozen peas into some boiling salted water. Peas cook faster than you think. They're better with a little crunch than mushy.

That's all there is to it. When you're done, rinse your plate, glass, fork, and knife and leave 'em in the sink for the next meal.

Oh, and if you can find your wife's hiding place for the Pinwheel cookies, they make a pretty good dessert—not as good as fresh rhubarb pie, but good enough for a batching cowboy.

BOOKS

Twenty-nine books in the *Hank the Cowdog* series (Maverick Books) and fourteen nonfiction books about Western life, published by the University of Nebraska Press, Maverick Books, Gulf Publishing Company, and the University of North Texas Press.

Dan Flores

*Dan Flores writes both scholarly
environmental history and books
for general audiences. His works have centered
on the exploration of the West, including his
own personal exploration.*

Dan Flores

Because he was born in Louisiana and now lives most of the year in Montana, some might argue that Dan Flores is not a Texas writer. Maybe not, but aside from the fact that this is my book and I can define "Texas writer" however I see fit, thank you, Dan lived in the Panhandle's Llano Estacado region for many years and built a house—as in, with his own hands, *built* a house—on twelve acres of prairie on the south rim of Yellow House Canyon. He also wrote two definitive books about this overprivatized and therefore largely undiscovered part of the state.

Describing Blanco and Yellow House canyons, his feelings for the land are unequivocal:

> *So visualize these prairie canyons: opposing, friable rims of gray, pink, or white rock; a dotting of junipers and mesquites setting off walls and mound-shaped swells of wheat-colored grasslands; galleries of cottonwoods and willows and, true, introduced elms and salt-cedars threading the bottoms of the valleys. Standing detached from the walls are elegant, graceful mesas and buttes, their sides sweeping in unbroken line up from the canyon floor, their tabletop peaks exactly on the level of the plain above. There are places, in Yellow House, in Blanco particularly, where I have stood on the rim, or a mesa top, and in my mind raced golden autumn light bareback across and into country so rounded and feminine smooth that I experienced profound sensual arousal.*

Those words were written by a man who does not, out of familiarity and dull-witted habit, take the landscape for granted. How then, could he abandon her for the north country? The answer is complicated but involves the scarcity of public lands in Texas. Although a few, relatively small state-owned chunks of land are open to the public, vast stretches—

beautiful, desirable stretches—are behind barbed-wire walls. For a man in love, this denied access became more than he could tolerate. Still, though, he loves her from a distance, and when he talks about the Llano Estacado, his eyes soften and his lips part slightly in a secret smile.

Dan Flores

I EAT, THEREFORE I AM

Before the orbiting space station, the Gatling gun, the Mayan *Popol Vuh,* the execution of the cave paintings at Lascaux—indeed, before the tool or even the word—there was sex, sleep, and eating. And of course you know only too well that, unlike the great bulk of our most cherished productions of culture, which go obsolete in the wink of a glare, the holy triad is with us still, a thinly veiled reminder that, despite our lavish veneer, at base none of us is anything but a smart monkey, waving an erection and a stick of sugarcane at the world, hoping for the best. Come dine with me, *mon cheri,* and we will all the basic pleasures prove. (I derive—outright theft is the more apt description—the imagery here from a photograph in that most illuminating magazine, *Natural History* [1997].)

If food and eating were that simple and direct a legacy, we'd most certainly today all be dining yet on platters of jungle fruits garnishing entrees of sugarcane, Mickey D's would be Mickey C's, and that invitation to dinner at seven would be way less obscured by culturality than it is now. But—to extrapolate from Michel Foucault and his *History of Sexuality*—what sexuality is to sex, food is to eating. The acts themselves lie at the heart of the matter, but what piles up after that are some of the very things that make our long, strange trip out of chimphood so fascinating. And entertaining.

I eat, therefore I am; but just about everything that I eat *by preference* (you have to ignore the odd anomaly, say the Donner Party, in this kind of analysis) depends on *who* I am. More specific to my situation, what I eat also depends on how far the nearest restaurant is (unluckily for my present situation, distant) and whether I can cook anything at all when left to my own devices. Let me take these one at a time and extrapolate toward some clarity before I grow so bold as to offer a suggestion as to what you might eat that I know how to make.

If food is culture, then like most of us I ought to be a maniacal miracle of multiculturalism. Perhaps unfortunately for Flores cuisine, though, the most nuanced ethnicity in my family comes from the male line. My dad's family represents the Louisiana-Texas interface at its most riotous, a real blending of cultural couplings that basically unfolded this way: A second-generation Spanish ancestor (whose father had been on hand at the founding of Los Adaes, the long-time Texas capital that now has evolved into a truck stop in Louisiana) married into a reasonably prominent French–Caddo Indian family whose roots lay in the Natchitoches area. Flores + Lafitte beget male descendants who eventually married (in successive generations) Italian, Dutch, and Anglo wives. Judging from what I grew up eating, it must have been the wives who did the cooking at every cycle. Amidst the soul food my mother learned to cook from her Arkansas and (Southern, damn it) Illinois ancestors, all that survived from that old original Spanish-French alliance were the following: the memory of a fondness for peppers and (the *creme* of my ethnic heritage) squirrel gumbo. Cat squirrel, preferably, since fox squirrels can be so tough, don't you know. With lots of red peppers. I still recall with some nostalgia the musical accompaniment—*ping, ping, ping*—of #6 shot coming to final rest as Dad made his way through a bowl of squirrel gumbo with the supreme satisfaction that all was right with the world.

Not another dish, though, came down from the rich ethnicity of that Louisiana heritage. Not boudin. Not etouffee. Foods whose origins lay south of the Pyrenees on the Iberian Peninsula? I was with my Dad the first time in his life he ate Mexican food, at the La Fonda in Santa Fe. It was 1985, and he was then sixty-nine years old. He asked the waiter (who to his credit never blinked an eye) for an order of "these fa-JEE-tas." When he was finished he belched and said that everything on the plate had tasted the same to him. He did enjoy the peppers.

By all that's inherited, then, I ought to offer up here a recipe for good ole Louisiana cat squirrel gumbo surrounded by collard greens, sweet potatoes wading in brown sugar and butter, and gravy with some biscuits under there somewhere. Washed down with iced tea, of course. That I'm not is no refutation of authentic legacy. I hope you understand that. What I eat is homage to my own life's journey, which has involved a good bit of remembering, a world's worth of learning, and just a bit of experimentation with the outer limits. Something old, something new, something borrowed, something with El Tesoro añejo in it.

So. In honor of ancestry, place, and all you can accrue waving sticks at the world, a favorite recipe of my adult trajectory through life is Green Chile Buffalo Pósole—a dish, as I see it, possible only from the cultural riot of the Southwest, since nearly every ingredient comes from a different historical tradition. For the proper release of all those ingredients into full sensuousness, Green Chile Buffalo Pósole should be washed down with another favorite—the simplest and most elegant, all-natural margarita known to the Southwest and points *way* north up the Rockies, where I now do most of my eating. (Note: I have to give proper credit, since I had my girlfriend fax me her remembered litany of the full range of ingredients here, which may be the ancestral tendency again but also might have something to do with making the margarita first. Make the margarita *last*.)

Here's what you need to make Green Chile Buffalo Pósole happen:

12 oz. of Indian pósole corn
2 quarts of water
2 lbs. of buffalo tenderloin steak sliced to bite-sized chunks
1 large garlic head, minced
3 fresh green chile peppers, variety and heat depending on how
    far outside the Southwest your origins lie
1 small white onion, chopped
1 tsp. of cumin
$\frac{1}{2}$ tsp. of oregano
1 red chile pepper, for color mostly
salt and pepper
cilantro for garnish

Prepare this way: Soak the pósole in water for a couple of hours to help soften the kernels. Meanwhile, build a campfire (with mesquite if it's available) and let it burn to coals. Keep a piñon log or two to throw on at the end, for proper olfactory stimulation. (Okay, a stove top will do, in a pinch, for the above, and you can always burn piñon incense.) Simmer the buffalo tenderloin chunks in butter and garlic in a covered pan. As the buffalo is browning, pour your water into a four-quart stock pan and add the pósole, the remaining garlic, the green chiles, the onion, the red pepper, the cumin and oregano, and a teaspoon of salt. Stir. Bring to a boil. When the buffalo tenderloin is cooked to medium rare, add it to the stock pan, cover the whole, and allow to simmer. Most white pósole will open fully in about 2 to 3 hours; blue corn pósole may take as long as 4 to 5 hours. Add salt and pepper to taste. Wave whatever is necessary to invite someone over. Ladle into soup bowls and garnish with cilantro.

The margaritas? Even simpler. The rule is 2-2-2: two medium-sized fresh limes, squeezed; two shots of Triple Sec; two shots of El Tesoro añejo tequila.

The great things about pósole, of course, are that (1) anyone can make it, (2) once you get it going, it requires little other than occasional stirring, (3) cooking it is like an incense of the Southwest, perfuming any setting whether inside or around a camp, and (4) it is better (and hotter) the second and third days than it is the first. All of us already know about the great things that follow from the sudden release of forty to fifty years of repressed sexual energy. I'm talking about the flowering of the agave plant to produce fine tequila, of course.

The morning I wrote this, a sterling spring dawn was breaking in the northern Rocky Mountains, one of the kind of days that produce a rose alpenglow in the high snowfields while dawn birds are singing from foothills sagebrush still in deep shadow. I was up early, thinking about pósole but also eyeballing striped Jupiter and the Galilean moons through a 200X telescope, marveling at the beauty and wondering about recent speculations that beneath the cracked ice sheets of Europa there is an ocean—and life.

Teeming life, maybe. Probably resting. Having sex. Resting again. And eating only the gods know what.

BOOKS

Jefferson and Southwestern Exploration. Norman: University of Oklahoma Press, 1984.

Journal of an Indian Trader: Anthony Glass and the Texas Trading Frontier, 1790–1810. College Station: Texas A&M University Press, 1985.

Canyon Visions: Photographs and Pastels of the Texas Plains (with Amy Gormley Winton). Lubbock: Texas Tech University Press, 1989.

Caprock Canyonlands: Journey into the Heart of the Southern Plains. Austin: University of Texas Press, 1990.

Mississippi Kite. Austin: University of Texas Press, 1993.

Jean Flynn

Jean Flynn writes biographies of famous
Texans for young adults. With more than
twenty-two years in public education, she now
enjoys a busy lecture series, conducting work-
shops for teachers and librarians.

Jean Flynn

When you are with Jean Flynn and her husband and fellow writer Bob Flynn, you understand why some marriages endure for reasons other than a couple's inertia. Jean and Bob don't smile at each other. They share a smile. They don't laugh at each other's anecdotes, they share eye-twinkling laughter, even though they know the punch lines. They don't look at each other, they exchange a look that makes others turn away out of respect for their privacy.

It is easy to understand why Bob Flynn is smitten with his wife. Besides being beautiful, she is also feminine in the most enviable sense of that word. She's a great cook—everyone says so—and when you're invited to a party at their house, you go, because the Flynns give parties that are relaxed and noisy. Like a turn at musical chairs, people nonchalantly position themselves to sit beside her at dinner parties, because she's smart and funny, and because she's a good listener. Looking up at you—she's shorter than most grownups, so she's usually looking up—she focuses on what you're saying as if it really were fabulously interesting. You leave feeling like you are, indeed, someone important.

Jean Flynn's

ROADKILL DINNERS

Wild game is a specialty around our house because after hunting season we can't afford anything else. But cooking the game is a natural for me. Dad was a sharecropper in Northwest Texas, which means he owned nothing but a passel of kids—six of his own and two orphaned nephews. When he could, he brought home rabbit, squirrel, frogs, or fish. He had an aversion to opossum and armadillo.

My parents never turned anyone away at mealtimes. Mama could stretch a meal farther than anyone I have ever known, simply by adding more milk or water to the gravy and making the biscuits a little smaller. Or I've seen her add more dumplings to the pot where a squirrel or rabbit had cooked off the bones.

But, becoming a big-city person, I have tried to sophisticate my cooking as well as myself. One of the things I have not changed and recommend to anyone who is cooking wild game is to let the meat drain thoroughly before doing anything with it. If meat has been frozen, I let it thaw in a colander (with a pan under it, of course) in the refrigerator. Now the meat will smell, so wrap the whole thing in a tightly closed plastic bag to keep from getting nauseated when you open the refrigerator door. Once you discard the juices from the meat, it will smell just like it was store-bought. One of my sophisticated recipes follows.

Burgundy Venison

2 lbs. venison, round (cut into one-inch cubes)
1 garlic clove (minced)
3 medium onions (diced)
4 tbs. butter or margarine (I use canola oil)
Salt, pepper, flour
$\frac{1}{4}$ tsp. marjoram
$\frac{1}{4}$ tsp. oregano
$\frac{1}{2}$ cup burgundy wine (I use chilled, so I can sip as I cook)
1 cup sour cream (I use nonfat)
4 oz. can mushrooms (drained unless you need to thin gravy)

Tenderize cubed venison and set aside. Sauté garlic, onions, and butter (or oil) until soft and brown. Remove onions and garlic from pan. Brown venison slowly in drippings. Return onions and garlic to pan. Add flour and water to thicken gravy (and to make as much as you want). Add salt and pepper to taste. Simmer $1\frac{1}{2}$ hours (covered but stir occasionally). Add mushrooms, herbs and wine. Simmer 15 minutes. Add sour cream and serve over wild rice (or plain white rice). Serves six.

When I was growing up, we ate what was on the table and then asked, "What was it?" But in the sophisticated world we now live in, some people who have been invited to a Roadkill Dinner at our house ask, "What is it?" before they take a bite. Or the really sophisticated ask, "What are you going to serve?" before they will accept an invitation to dinner.

We occasionally have buffet dinners for as many as sixty guests. I always prepare one store-bought meat for those who get sick at the thought of eating wild game. One guest at a Christmas party was so suspicious that the only thing he would eat was turkey. It was the only wild thing on the table. That was several years ago, and today if he were told that he ate wild game, he would throw up just to prove his point.

Our wild-game dishes range from a rattlesnake appetizer (depending on the last time Bob stepped on one) to sweet-and-sour venison meatballs (depending on Bob's luck the last time he went hunting) to barbecued pork (depending on the last time Bob ran over a wild hog), with a host of others in between. All wild game should be served with squash or eggplant casserole, twice-baked potatoes, corn pie, pinto beans, and jalapeño cornbread, topped by some kind of Texas pecan dessert.

And to show how sophisticated I have become, we eat by bamboo torch light under the trees by the patio. That way guests can't see what they are eating and have to wait to ask, "What was it?"

Even in a sophisticated world, everything in life goes full circle.

BOOKS

Jim Bowie: A Texas Legend. Austin, Tex.: Eakin Press, 1980.

Stephen F. Austin: The Father of Texas. Austin, Tex.: Eakin Press, 1981.

William Barret Travis: Victory or Death! Austin, Tex.: Eakin Press, 1982.

James Butler Bonham: The Rebel Hero. Austin, Tex.: Eakin Press, 1983.

James Walker Fannin: Remember Goliad! Austin, Tex.: Eakin Press, 1985.

Lady: The Story of Claudia Alta (Lady Bird) Johnson. Austin, Tex.: Eakin Press, 1992.

Anson Jones: The Last President of the Republic of Texas. Austin, Tex.: Eakin Press, 1996.

VIDEOS

Heroes of the Texas Revolution. Matson Multi-Media, 1994.

The Spanish Missions of Texas. Matson Multi-Media, 1995.

Robert Flynn is an accomplished author of novels and short stories, for which he has won numerous awards. He also has published a nonfiction book about the Vietnam War.

Robert Flynn

I'm a member of a group of professional women who meet once a month to discuss common concerns. So that our gatherings won't sink into gossip sessions, we decide on a topic for each session. ("Session" is not a slip; these are essentially group therapy sessions for clench-jawed overachievers.) Awhile back, our assignment was to describe desirable qualities in a friend. We talked about things like kindness and helpfulness and reliability; however, a quality that I considered to be just as important was being a good conversationalist. When pressed on what, exactly, I meant by that, I set about describing Bob Flynn:

"First of all, he has to have a sense of humor. This is not a raunchy or slapstick sense of humor, but rather the ability to be amused (sometimes bemused) by what is going on around him. Next, he must be able to keep up with at least two, but better three, threads of conversation—sometimes completely unrelated—at the same time. During the conversation, he is able to interlace the threads with running jokes and word plays and sidelong thoughts. The person has to be interested in stuff. Just about all stuff. Interested people are interesting people. Most important, the person must never seem to be stretching to be clever, while, in reality, accomplish just that. This cleverness requires an enormous amount of easygoing attention to what is being said to him."

Robert Flynn's
LION STEW
(FOR THE LION-HEARTED)

The way to Ewaso Ngiro was so rough I bounced off the seat and bumped my head on the roof of the vehicle. It was so rough my wife said the thing she most regretted not bringing to Africa was a jogging bra. Led by our Kikuyu guide, we were driving into Masai territory, into an area few non-Masai ever saw.

This was not a Kenya game reserve. This was the Ewaso Ngiro Plain, unmarked by roads. Masai herdsmen watched us pass, as did herds of zebra, impala, and wildebeest. We drove across the plain until we reached a riverine acacia forest on the edge of the Loita Hills. The Bantu drivers guided the truck and two vans around acacia, thornbush, and deep holes left by anteaters, and stopped in a thicket.

Two vultures watched our arrival with veiled interest. Sunlight filtered dimly through the trees. The earth was invisible beneath high grass and low bushes. I looked out the window in disbelief. This couldn't be our campsite; this was jungle.

As a native Texan, I had an in-bred suspicion of brush and high grass that could harbor centipedes, scorpions, spiders, and snakes. Most snakes, I knew, were nonpoisonous, in Texas. In Kenya, the only nonpoisonous snake was the python.

When John Ochieng, our guide, told us to get out, I, like the others, left my belongings inside the vehicle. I wasn't convinced this was going to be our camp until the drivers dumped the tents on the ground and the cooks, armed with machetes, chopped a "kitchen" out of the undergrowth beneath a tree.

Ochieng, who spoke fluent English, Swahili, and several tribal dialects, led us around the campground to put us at ease. He was a teacher, naturalist, and survival instructor; and he gave us English and Swahili names for the birds, trees, and bushes and laughed at our concern about snakes in the high grass. "Go slow and single file," he advised us. "They'll get out of your way. If you crowd up and trap them between you, they'll coil and strike."

I joined the end of the single file as Ochieng led us on a hike to a spring and along the river. Weaver nests hung from the trees. A yellow-billed stork waded in the shallow water. It was a peaceful scene, and when we returned, camp didn't seem so hostile. Ochieng pointed out the toilets—men to the left of the tents, women to the right, no one toward the spring, and all tissue paper was to be brought back to camp and burned. Ochieng also was an ecologist.

Under his direction, we set up our tents in a close semicircle and rolled out our sleeping bags. The tent was of the utilitarian variety. It was high enough that I could crawl in, long enough that I could stretch out my full six feet, and wide enough for two intimate friends and one duffel bag. It contained the essentials—a fly for deflecting rain; netting for keeping out flies and mosquitoes; a floor to provide separation, if not total protection, from water, scorpions, ants, and snakes; and canvas sides that were impervious to lions. That was what Ochieng assured us. And he was an experienced guide and survival instructor.

Ochieng suffered from a recurrence of malaria, and, after inspecting the location of the tents, he went to sleep, telling us that we could explore the area as long as we did not go alone, told the others where we were going, and kept in the clearings and away from the bush. My wife and I walked out of the forest to explore the plains. Masai cattle kept the grass short, and we avoided the occasional thickets. We saw ring-necked doves, rabbits, and dik-dik. We picked up two skulls and three jawbones and tried to identify the animals they had belonged to. Two Masai wearing red togas and beaded necklaces, and carrying clubs and short stabbing spears, began following us. They shouted, waved, and made gestures which we interpreted as warning us away from something, perhaps their herds. We returned to the camp.

Two other Masai, who looked like teenage boys, came to the camp to stare curiously at our pale faces. The Masai, who have little body hair, felt the hair on my forearm. A young woman with shoulder-length brunette hair drew their attention. They touched her hair and examined it with their fingers. One of the young men had two wives, five children, and 150 cattle and was interested in the brunette for a third wife.

The brunette, who was going to be a teaching assistant at Ohio State University in the fall, believed her father would be flattered at the offer of 150 cattle, until one of the drivers explained that the Masai had not offered all his cattle. Negotiation with her father was still to take place. The brunette abandoned the courtship and withdrew to her tent.

After the Masai left, I walked a short distance behind the tents and watched the sun set through the flat-topped thorn trees. The sky went blue, to pink, to orange, to crimson; and the insects and long-tailed hoepoes went quiet.

Before the sky turned to black, I joined the others at the folding tables the cooks had set up in a clearing they had hacked out between our tents and the cook area. John Mbogo, chief cook, brought lentil soup, which was salty but delicious. The soup was always salty but delicious. I had almost finished mine when a lion roared just beyond the cook area. The cooks and drivers reassembled at our table, grabbing our lanterns and pointing flashlights at the bushes on three sides of the kitchen. Mbogo saw a lion beside the truck that carried the food and tents.

It wasn't the presence of the lions that was frightening; it was the fact that the cooks and drivers were scared. They started two roaring bonfires, one near our table and the other near the kitchen. Mbogo had two flashlights in one hand and appropriated mine because it was more powerful.

"We know the lions in the game reserves," he explained. "We know what they'll do. These lions aren't used to people. We don't know what they'll do." He played the flashlight beams on the darkness beyond the dim light of the lanterns.

A lion was in heavy brush, and all we could see was the glitter of his eye, first one eye and then the other, as the head moved through the brush. The lion was walking toward us. While Mbogo and I watched the glittering eye, a big lioness walked through the beam of the flashlight. The lioness was twenty yards away, and as soon as she disappeared into the darkness, Mbogo and I backed up to the fire.

We turned for advice to Ochieng, who was drowsing at the table. He assured us that the lions would not come into the camp with all of us yelling and running around, and that lions would not come into the tents. We searched the darkness with our flashlights for several minutes and then gathered around the fire. It took longer for the cooks to return to the cook fire, because the kitchen had brush on three sides. While Mbogo finished dinner, Elijah watched.

Mbogo and Elijah brought fresh salad, sweet and sour pork, and fresh corn and peas to the table, but we were slow to settle down enough to eat. We all wanted to tell what we had seen or heard. Only a few of us had seen the lions, but everyone had heard them. No one was certain how many lions there had been, but Mbogo thought there were two lionesses and some younger lions.

I had scarcely tasted my dessert of fresh fruit cocktail when a lion roared from the bush outside the kitchen. We deserted the table again to look for the lions. I'm not sure why we were looking for the lions, but the cooks and drivers ran from one side of the camp area to the other flashing their lights on the darkness, so we joined them. I think no one wanted to see the lions, but everyone wanted to know where they were.

A lion roared on the other side of the camp. They had circled and were now behind our tents. The cooks and drivers threw wood on both fires, and we returned to the table, fetched our chairs, and dragged them to the blaze. We finished dessert and took our coffee or hot chocolate and huddled around the fire. The evening was cool, but we huddled more for spiritual than physical comfort.

We sat by the fire, watching our backs and trying to scare each other. Ochieng slept in his chair. He roused from time to time to assure us that lions would not come into tents, and in an act of mercy we insisted that he go to bed, as he had a high fever.

We lingered by the fire, drinking coffee and hot chocolate, listening to the lions that had stilled the other sounds of the night. No one really wanted to go to bed. We enjoyed our coffee, one another's company, and the roaring of the lions. No one wanted to walk to his or her tent alone.

After a time the women organized a trip to the powder room and trooped off together. I watched them leave with some disappointment. My wife was among them, which meant that I would walk to the tent alone. After a few jokes about women traveling in herds, we men said goodnight and manfully walked alone. I talked the whole way to the other men, who were also talking. I wanted everyone to know where I was, and my mouth prepared to scream.

I zipped up the mosquito netting but left the outside covering open so that I could see. I couldn't see the lions, but they got so close Mbogo drove a vehicle behind the tents to drive them away.

I went to sleep and was awakened by the roar of a lion that sounded like it was between our tent and the kitchen. My wife and I got out of our bags to look through the mosquito netting but could see nothing. We could, however, hear it padding behind the tent. Then we heard one of the vehicles start and drive behind the tents. After that, we heard the lions but never again so close.

As early as two o'clock, I regretted the two cups of coffee mocha I had enjoyed in the camaraderie of the campfire. By three o'clock I was in heavy internal debate as to the prudence of leaving the tent. By three-thirty I was envisioning the headlines I would make after being dragged away by a lion while attending nature's call. Was that the way I wanted my life to end, a victim of healthy kidneys? By four o'clock the debate was over, but I didn't go far; with one hand I kept the flashlight beam making a constant, if not steady, 360-degree sweep.

I was up early the next morning, eager to recount the sounds of the night over a cup of coffee. As recompense for waking my wife during the night to ask her to listen for any strangled screams or sounds of a heavy body being dragged through the brush, I promised to bring her a cup of coffee in bed. However, I was the first one up. The cooks and drivers had abandoned their tents and were asleep in the vehicles. Only we tourists had known the security of the canvas tents.

I sat in one of the camp chairs and relished the tranquillity of the morning. I revived the fire and thought over the excitement of the night and the adventure of the day to come. And the lions that would return at nightfall. I decided I liked it. I decided I would be disappointed if the lions didn't return. I decided to limit all liquids after four o'clock in the afternoon and no coffee after dinner.

Ingredients:
two lbs. of diced lion or other hearty meat (fat trimmed)
two cans of non-fat chicken broth
two large cubed potatoes
two large sliced carrots
one large sliced onion
two cans of Rotel diced tomatoes with jalapeño peppers
one can of whole kernel corn
one can of beans
one tablespoon Worcestershire sauce
pepper and Mrs. Dash (extra spicy) to taste

Boil water in a Dutch oven. Lots of water. Length of boiling time is determined by the cleanliness of the Dutch oven. If you are cooking at home, and your hands and pans are clean, you may dispense with this step.

Dispatch a lion. Note: venison, elk, buffalo, or beef may be substituted. If beef is substituted, dispatch your own cow or obtain meat from a licensed butcher.

Cube two pounds of lion meat, preferably back-strap or hindquarter. Let meat drain thoroughly.

Put the meat in the dutch oven. Add two cans of chicken broth and simmer until the meat is tender.

Add two cans of Rotel diced tomatoes with jalapeño peppers and liquid from a can of green beans and a can of whole kernel corn. Add cut onion, potatoes, and carrots and simmer until the vegetables are tender.

Add remaining green beans and whole kernel corn, a tablespoon of Worcestershire sauce, black pepper, and Mrs. Dash (extra spicy) to taste.

Simmer, stirring frequently to prevent sticking, until stew has reached desired thickness.

Refrigerate for two days, heat, and serve.

Served with hot cornbread, recipe will serve six. Can be frozen.

BOOKS

North to Yesterday. Fort Worth: Texas Christian University Press, 1985.

Seasonal Rain. San Antonio, Tex.: Corona, 1986.

Wanderer Springs. Fort Worth: Texas Christian University Press, 1987.

A Personal War in Vietnam. College Station: Texas A&M University Press, 1989.

The Sounds of Rescue, the Signs of Hope. Fort Worth: Texas Christian University Press, 1989.

In the House of the Lord. Fort Worth: Texas Christian University Press, 1991.

When I Was Just Your Age. Denton: University of North Texas Press, 1992.

Living with the Hyenas. Fort Worth: Texas Christian University Press, 1995.

The Last Klick. Dallas: Basset Books, 1996.

*Kinky Friedman is former leader of the band
The Texas Jewboys. After a wild stint in New
York City, he now lives on a quiet ranch in the
Texas Hill Country where he writes internation-
ally acclaimed mystery novels and spoils his pets.*

Kinky Friedman

The physicians' dining room at the hospital where I work is hardly a chirpy place to have lunch. In fact, unless another woman physician is present to break the drone of men discussing—expletives deleted—the pros and cons of managed care, the evils of medical malpractice plaintiff attorneys, and the best ways to get rid of fire ants and oak decline, I usually eat my lunch pretty fast and make tracks. ("Hate to run, guys, but I'm burning daylight. See y'all.")

A recent and notable exception was the day we got off on Kinky Friedman. I don't recall how it started, but within minutes, all four tables full of doctors were shouting their favorite song lyrics and one-liners and Kinky stories. They even got into a debate over the Kinkster's views on women.

"Did you hear about how the National Organization of Women awarded him the Male Chauvinist Pig of the Year Award after he recorded 'Get Your Biscuits in the Oven and Your Buns in the Bed?'"

"Yep, those women just didn't get it, though. Kinky was making fun of male chauvinists, for chrissake."

"Well, I'm not so sure. Anyone who would write a song about wanting a waitress to come sit on his face . . . "

There was so much whooping and shouting and general merry-making that I was afraid someone was going to knock on our door and ask us to keep it down. There are, after all, sick people in the hospital. But, gosh, it sure was fun.

Kinky Friedman's
CHICKEN McGOVERN

(An excerpt from *The Love Song of J. Edgar Hoover.* Used by permission of International Creative Management, Inc. Copyright © 1996 by Kinky Friedman.)

It was a clear, crisp, beautiful Friday night in the city sometime around the middle of April and McGovern was having an intimate dinner party at his place which, I am not terribly shocked to report, was back to its usual state of comfortable disarray. McGovern's guest list that evening was limited to three: Beverly, Stephanie DuPont, and myself. The dish he was serving, which he'd labored all afternoon to prepare, was his famous, incomparable Chicken McGovern.

"That was the best chicken I've ever had in my life," said Stephanie, across the candlelight and chicken bones. "You've got to tell me how to make it."

"It's an Old World recipe," said McGovern. "It's rather complicated. For about thirty years I've kept it right up here." McGovern pointed to his very large and handsome head, but Stephanie, being young and impetuous, still wasn't satisfied.

"If it's not a secret," she said like a petulant child, "why can't I borrow it? Surely you've got the recipe written down somewhere."

"Stephanie," I said, "if McGovern doesn't want to give away his recipe he doesn't want to give away his recipe. You wouldn't dream of walking up to Colonel Sanders and asking him to give you his eleven different secret herbs and spices."

"First of all," said Stephanie, "I wouldn't be walking up to Colonel Sanders. He'd probably be crawling up to me and asking for my telephone number. Secondly, Mike McGovern can cook absolute circles around Colonel Sanders."

She favored McGovern with a stunning, admiring smile of such intensity that it could've launched a thousand cookbooks and floated them all the way to Troy. Basking in the afterglow, McGovern got up from the table and wandered into the kitchen, where he could be seen picking up a steak knife and prying loose a board under the sink. His three dinner guests looked on in mild amazement.

"There's a hidden compartment here," said McGovern, "where I keep my old recipes and stuff. I haven't opened it in years and I can't promise, but if I was a hard copy of Chicken McGovern, this is where I'd be."

"He's such an accommodating host," I clucked approvingly.

"I never knew that hidden compartment was there," said Beverly.

"That's what makes it a hidden compartment," said McGovern, as he extracted a sheaf of yellowed papers and proceeded to shake the dust and cobwebs off into the trash.

"He always ceases to amaze me," I said, as I lit an afterdinner cigar to the disapproving eye of Stephanie. But the main focus of the dinner guests was now clearly upon McGovern.

"Holy shit," he said, looking over the recipes.

"What?" I said.

"Now I remember where I got the recipe," said McGovern. "I memorized it so long ago that I'd forgotten. Leaning Jesus gave it to me."

"WHAT!" Stephanie and I shouted simultaneously.

Before Beverly could say "Who's Leaning Jesus?" the two of us were on our feet waiting as McGovern trundled the ancient document over to the table.

"Let me have a look," said Stephanie. "A girl knows about these things."

She gave McGovern another stunner of a smile and he put the recipe in her rapacious hands. I got up and put on my reading skepticals and walked around behind her as she sat back down to read the recipe. The ingredients and instructions were as follows:

The Marinade

three or four pound chicken cut up with backbone and wingtips
    used for stock
fresh ginger
three scallions diced finely
drumsticks, thighs, and white meat scored, skinned, and cleaned
    of hidden fat pockets
two tsp roasted browned peppercorns
two TB soy sauce
sugar sprinkled to taste

The Sauce

four garlic cloves diced finely and mashed
four scallions diced finely
one stalk celery
a few stems fresh coriander or parsley
fresh grated ginger to taste
two TB light soy sauce
two tsp distilled white vinegar
four TB chicken stock
one TB tomato ketchup
sugar to taste
two TB sesame oil

You Also Require

cornstarch for dredging
nonfat oil for deep frying
toasted peanuts to taste

Putting It Together

Peel and grate the ginger finely.
Dice scallions into very fine rounds.
Divide chicken and put into bowl.
Score or prick with a sharp knife.
Sprinkle with ground peppercorns, ginger, scallions, soy sauce, and
   sugar.
Rub in well with hands.
Cover and refrigerate for four hours or overnight.

For the Sauce, Use Two Separate Bowls

In one bowl place the mashed garlic, diced scallions, and celery cut
   into very fine rounds.
Mash ginger and cut into minute dice.
Combine and set aside.

In the other bowl, stir well soy sauce, vinegar, stock, ketchup,
   sugar, and sesame oil.
Set aside.

After chicken is marinated, set in a row and dust all over with
  cornstarch.
Pat chicken until mixture is well absorbed.
Set aside for twenty minutes.
Fry in hot vegetable oil until crusty.
Bake in oven at 350 degrees for thirty to forty minutes, dependent
  upon size of chicken pieces.
Drain on paper towel and place on serving dish.

Mix together the two bowls of sauce ingredients and bathe the
  chicken.

Sprinkle with toasted peanuts.
Open mouth.
Serve at once.

"Wait a minute," said Stephanie. "There's one more page to this."
"It's already the longest recipe in the world," I said.

It was also just about the most disappointing recipe in the world, I
thought, as I poured myself a very generous portion of brandy and
drifted over to the wall above the empty fireplace to share my sorrows
with Carole Lombard. Sometimes, I reflected rather grimly, no matter who wrote it, who cooks it, who serves it, or who eats it, a recipe
is just a recipe.

BOOKS

Greenwich Killing Time. New York: Beechtree Books, 1986.
A Case of Lone Star. New York: Beechtree Books, 1987.
When the Cat's Away. New York: Beechtree Books, 1988.
Frequent Flyer. New York: Morrow, 1989.
Musical Chairs. New York: Morrow, 1991.
The Kinky Friedman Crime Club. London, Boston: Faber & Faber, 1992.
Elvis, Jesus, and Coca Cola. New York, Simon & Schuster, 1993.
Armadillos and Old Lace. New York: Simon & Schuster, 1994.
God Bless John Wayne. New York: Simon & Schuster, 1995.
The Love Song of J. Edgar Hoover. New York: Simon & Schuster, 1996.
Roadkill. New York: Simon & Schuster, 1997.

Lionel G. Garcia has received numerous awards for his novels including the PEN Southwest Discovery Prize and the Texas Institute of Letters Best Novel Award. During the day he practices veterinary medicine in Seabrook.

Lionel G. Garcia

Lionel Garcia writes about Mercé, his insane uncle: "I remember how his fits would start, sensing his changing mood, how with one hand he would yank at his ears because he heard voices that ordered him to curse and who to curse, dragging me with the other around town. Some days, while he held me in his arms and took off with me I felt there would be no end to his fits and that we were forever destined to pull at our ears and curse at the whole town."

Lionel Garcia is a practicing veterinarian, a husband of thirty-eight years, the father of three fine children and grandfather of one, the author of award-winning books, and a prized public speaker. Because of all these clinical indicators to the contrary, I feel comfortable asking him if he has inherited any of that craziness. (I know, I know. That was an impolite question. My mother has taught me better; however, my father, a retired psychiatrist, says it's okay to ask people if they're crazy. It minimizes tedious chit-chat.) Politeness and expediency aside, I asked him about the state of his mind because of his choice of possessive pronouns: "We were forever destined to pull at *our* ears."

Dr. Garcia isn't offended in the least by the question and answers, laughing, "I know I am, because craziness runs in my family. But, I have learned to compensate. My writing keeps me sane." Dr. Garcia goes on to say that the person whom his friends see is not the same person who writes, spiraling deep into his brain. He even talks about his writing self in the third person, as if he were talking about a curious stranger who inhabits his body. He describes fiction writing as being as intense as an out-of-body experience and admits that later he may read something that he has written and be embarrassed by the intimacy and candor of his words. In some cases, he may not even remember writing the words.

Truth told, aren't we all a little like Dr. Garcia's uncle? Don't we all, from time to time, hear voices that tell us to do the equivalent of cursing at the whole town? The only difference is that most of us don't actually do it. Some—Dr. Garcia, for instance—sit down at a desk and place their fingers on a keyboard.

Lionel G. Garcia's
MASA
(TAKEN FROM WRITINGS OF SEVERAL MEXICAN NOVELISTS)

I am sorry that I do not have an original recipe since my ancestors as well as I were and I am still too poor to eat. I do have, from some old archives I came across in Mexico, the following recipe which I submit with the idea not so much of giving you the procedure as much as giving you the idea.

Corn: (One sack.) Corn of my ancestors, corn of the people who have come before me and you, and you, you are in the corn, the corn that is the seed of all that is in the civilization before us. One seed! Conqueror of the world. Your seed, one seed, that has borne the countless generations before us and fed us with the germination of your miracle of ideas and pulpy substance. Corn. Corn. The Corn of my Father: (Any older man.) and your father, your mother: (Any old woman.) and her mother until there is no one to talk to, except the corn and its husk, the husk of life, that gives the life to the seed as my mother gave seed to me, implanted in the soil of her womb, her heavy innards moistened with the saliva of a thousand glands—No!—billions of glands, secretory symbols that in themselves create the grime of life, pasting the honeyed womb of my mother so that all of us, you, you can be attached to it and be nourished for life. Corn. Corn and something else, that something that brings to life that which in itself is not alive and yet not dead. Corn, to grind. Dry corn floating in a Tub: (Large tub.) Of lime water (five to ten gallons.) giving up your husks, like you give up your freedom, as a birth, floating as if mesmerized by the lime itself and all that is in your tub. Your tub, as we speak of your tub and its water and the floating of your dry corn surrendering all that is its cover. Exposed! To the world exposed and naked of your husk and baring your soul to be skimmed by the gentle hands of your sainted and apostolic Mother: (Same old woman.) and her mother and her mother and her mother. Will you stop? Will your mother stop? Will she continue as her mother has done before her? Corn! Now we have your corn! We call it *maize*. Now we have your corn in the bowels of her net and now we have the net in her gentle hands. To crush! Crush the corn, grinding away, as you grind away your sins from which you have protected your mother and your father and all your antecedents, forever glued to the virginous vulva of your sainted mother, separating her pubic hairs as the corn silk was separated, tearing away the maiden-headed leaves, as your father tore into her in the rages of his youth, reaching in and flicking away the worm, that which is verminous and foul inside the ephemeral existence of your greening form, just as he would have easily torn off your worm of existence, and just as he wormed his way into the line of ancestors before him, ancestors who would have rather died in the nakedness of their being rather than to have betrayed your soul, the protectors and procreators of your soul.

Father! Father, who harvested the corn and now rests on the loins of the world asleep, drugged by the feelings of the good harvest and the bad land. Asleep! Asleep in the drugged prescience of the world truly round, his head resting on the floor that was touched by the dust that flew across this earth from Calvary to secrete itself in the jointed space of your being and his eternal abode, drugged by the mystical powers of the dust of the dust of the dust of the dust of Calvary. Land! From the land to the harvest my father is the man responsible for: Mother, Corn, Land, Water, Lime, Tub. Who is to move the tub? Your man, of course. Man and father and son, combined in the unholy trinity of your responsibility, responsible to each of you for your alimentation, and his fornication, and your defecation. Your father, part man, part lion, part animal of the seas who in one blow could consume the universe by the strength of his forefathers, people who came and killed and conquered and stayed in the warmth of the fluids your mother was secreting on the day when there was no sun or moon and the heavens played just as children play with little mice on a purple string, your string of life, that individual string that you have tucked inside the navel of your spine, the end of which moves forever and ever as I wind it unto my pallid hand that has no more force than the sub-particles of life; even your force redefined could not force me to extend the string to visit the places where the heavens play, the Orlando and the Anaheim, on the contralateral side of the blackest of the black holes. Maybe Navy blue. Oh! The bluest of the navy blue of the blackest of the black holes, where they play on the day of no moon and no sun. Grinding the corn.

The corn. Seed of eternal countries. Life-blood of the world and all its beings. Feed the starved: of starvation and of the spirit. Move! There is no food there. Mother! Mother of eternal flames and bastard children who suck on the nipple of the soul of the universe twice formed! Mother, your mother. Your mother bent in shape bending over and grinding, bent over in the position that the antecedents *had* their women—over tubs and barrels—bent grinding, not knowing who or when this had been done before and at what age? Face somber: as somber as you when you are told there is no Santa Claus! No Santa Claus! And you run to your mother, bent over the tub of corn as it is being fed to the grinder of life, jaws of steel and cobalt whose existence presages the destruction of the universal corn, changing it into a shapeless shape, shape of no shape as our forefathers have no shape but continue to exist in the bowels of your father's perpetual skin, skin so tight that the fathers of all the antecedents were amazed that your father could, nay, would, urinate. And my mother and your mother—Yes, your mother—wondering: When will the corn be ready? In a day? Or two? What presages the corn? And what price do we pay? Leave it alone for days or weeks and let the rancidness over the days become the lifeblood of the husks to which it is returned once more to be filled with the bowels of so many animals that the mind reeks—rebels—when told.

Then is when you come to terms with the differentness of the mess which is to one what it is not to another or another or another, which is to say that no one knows what to do at the end except gather the neighborhood and say that you have done the deed again and that forgiveness is not in order but that all is work now until all is gone. And they sit around and talk about the inconsistency of life and seek egalitarianistic repercussions while all the time sucking on the reed of existence which produces only enough air for one or two to breathe. Slap and slap is heard amid the noise as the glue is prepared back to the husk from where it came. Lifeblood again and again—by the dozens—to be spread through the village with the good news that to-morrow has come and all is well again. One year has passed and I lay dying in this mess, spread against me, my body, by my enemies and friends, everyone that has a hand in this and cannot keep from doing so even as they try with all their might not to do so but revel in the thought of the dying encased in masa of my existence and yet I lay dying today when yesterday I felt quite well, enough to participate in my motherness and fatherness of this eternal tradition lest this custom should engulf the world.

BOOKS

Leaving Home. Houston: Arte Público Press, 1985.
A Shroud in the Family. Houston: Arte Público Press, 1987.
Hardscrub. Houston: Arte Público Press, 1990.
I Can Hear the Cowbells Ring. Houston: Arte Público Press, 1994.
To a Widow with Children. Houston: Arte Público Press, 1994.

STAGE PLAYS

An Acorn on the Moon. (Winner of Texas Playwright Festival, 1995)

John Graves lives and writes in Glen Rose.
He has received many awards for his
writing including a National Book Award
nomination for Goodbye to a River,
considered by many to be the best book
ever written by a Texan.

John Graves

When I saw that Don Graham had written a review essay about John Graves in the November 1996 issue of the *Texas Observer,* the first words out of my mouth were, "He better not have." Being familiar with Don Graham's irreverent flesh-tearings of Larry McMurtry, it was with my own claws extended that I turned to his article about John Graves. You have to understand, I spent four years of my life working on a book that I wasn't even sure anyone would publish just so that I might have a chance to somehow, possibly, maybe meet John Graves. I share the opinion of most other readers, at least those with two neurons working at the same time, that John Graves doesn't need a canoe to get down a river—he could just walk down the middle. Not to worry, though, I could retract my claws. Don Graham's remarks indicated that his neurons are working fine, since he places Mr. Graves on the same high ledge where I do.

As it turned out, my ruminations and writings were unnecessary. All I had to do in order to sit down and talk with this kind and very approachable man, was, well, sit down and talk. I didn't need a calling card or a letter of introduction or a published book to my credit. I had only to introduce myself, sit down beside him at the table where he was signing books, stammer a few inane remarks, blush, giggle shrilly, act like an utter idiot, get up, and stumble away. Nothing to it. Mr. Graves even told me what a pleasure it was to meet me and smiled as he shook my hand. I did, however, notice something unusual as I turned back to gaze upon him once more. The late afternoon sun, slanting through the long windows behind his chair, made a perfect circle of light around his head.

John Graves's

IDEAL RECIPE, BUT SELDOM ATTAINABLE SPECIAL SANDWICH

I got to pondering on that special sandwich of mine and came up with a sort of ideal recipe for it, seldom attainable. Also seldom edible by me now, unless I ignore certain medical prohibitions. It ought to be made in summer at the height of vegetable gardens' productivity, if a couple of ingredients are to serve their purpose fully. When constructed right, this sandwich calls for lots of paper napkins.

Bread: Home-made whole wheat. We used to grind our own flour for this, too, after winnowing the grain in front of an electric fan, but that was long ago. The best of this bread came from the magic hands of our older daughter, but she has lived on the upper East Coast for many years now, and we make do with an automatic breadmaking machine, which causes me some shame but not much.

Spreads: Non-crunchy peanut butter on one slice and mayonnaise on the other, plenty of both. The mayonnaise ought to be homemade, too, but seldom is these days.

Lettuce: Fresh Buttercrunch or another tender leaf sort, laid on the peanut butter side.

Tomatoes: Big Boy or Better Boy or some other of the juicy, full-flavored varieties, right off of the vine except for chilling, sliced thin and stacked up on the lettuce until the slices start sliding off.

Bacon: Several thick slices of the old, true, dry-cured, smokehouse kind, cooked on a flat griddle in a hot oven until crisp but not black or even dark brown. They ought to cover the tomatoes entirely.

Embellishments: On occasion, I used to put a hard-fried egg on top of the back but for some reason seldom do so anymore. Ditto for slivers of fresh green jalapeño, seeds attached.

BOOKS

Goodbye to a River. New York: Knopf, 1960.

Hard Scrabble. New York: Knopf, 1974.

The Last Running. Austin, Tex.: Encino Press, 1974.

Texas Heartland. College Station: Texas A&M University Press, 1975.

From a Limestone Edge. New York: Knopf, 1980.

Blue and Some Other Dogs. Austin, Tex.: Encino Press, 1981.

Of Birds and Texas. Fort Worth, Tex.: Gentliny Editions, 1986.

Self-Portrait with Birds. Dallas: Chama, 1991.

A John Graves Reader. Austin: University of Texas Press, 1996.

A. C. Greene is well known for his newspaper columns, essays, nonfiction books, and screenplays. He is a fellow of the Texas Institute of Letters and the Texas State Historical Association.

A. C. Greene

I've always thought it is impolite to ask someone who uses their initials just what exactly those initials stand for. I figure that if they preferred the name, they would use it instead of the initials. Having just met him and his wife Judy (and still within that narrow stage of familiarity when I was straining to be polite), I didn't ask A. C. Greene what the A and the C are covering up. (Adelbert, maybe, or Ambrose? How about Algernon?) Because Mr. Greene volunteered the information, though, I learned what "M. C. G." at the bottom of numerous paintings in his home stands for: Mark Cole Greene, Mr. Greene's second oldest of four children, an artist whose paintings are a bargain when they sell for seven hundred dollars apiece.

Like his father's writings, Mark's paintings have the equivalent of a distinctive voice, with uninhibited use of color and decisive, self-assured lines. Repetition of shapes gives the paintings harmony and fluidity, and most have a festive tone. Subjects include hot-air balloons, the cosmos, the *Titanic,* and intertwining vines alive with grinning tiger monkeys, arms outstretched.

In the mid-1950s, when Mark was born, the term being used for his specialness was "minimal brain injury." When I asked A. C. Greene to tell me about his experiences rearing a son with limitations, he admitted that there were challenges, but, without hesitation (or martyrdom), he added that he had learned something valuable from Mark—you must be able to bend. This patience and compassion is reflected in the many, many books that Mr. Greene has written or contributed to during his long writing career. His books are so numerous that I couldn't quite reach from where they start on one shelf and end on the next—even if I stretched like a tiger monkey.

A. C. Greene's stories explore the complexities and delicious ambiguities of human interactions. My favorite is a short story about his childhood, entitled "The Too-Big Christmas Tree." The story is about the marriage-defining conflict that developed between his parents over a tree that was too tall to fit in their living room. After angrily exploring various possibilities—including boring a hole in the living room floor—the tree eventually was "pushed into a ninety-degree bend against the ceiling a yard or so from its tip." Maybe it was then, as a small boy, Mr. Greene began to understand the family-melding importance of being able to bend.

A. C. Greene's

BEER STEAK AND KAHLÚA CHICKEN

I'd like to preface my recipes by admitting, I've not held title as a bestseller kitchen hand. I'm a decent salad maker, but not with the kind of dedication the balsamic vinegar and fresh basil people exhibit. I don't have a chapter on sauces in me—or even a paragraph. As for my pasta, I wouldn't sentence anyone to eat the contents, based on past pasta performance. That about covers it; so, I'm bound to say in words of one syllable, the stove is not my line. Period. But with that introduction, I proceed with *Beer Steak* and *Kahlúa Chicken,* though you will find neither on the pages or in the index of *Joy of Cooking.*

Let's do the beer steak first. Properly produced, this will be done outdoors. No, not on a deck or a porch: out-of-doors, the open sky, the stars at night, etc. For years I have used a big, old-fashioned iron wash pot, the kind roadside antique stores have hanging out front. I got mine from my dad as a "Welcome Home from the Wars" gift. Well, he said I could have it if I would drive to Dallas and pick up the pot. (That phrase mustn't be taken too literally; wrestle it around, maybe, but pick it up? Unnhuh.) Daddy said the pot had been in the Beeman family whose farm had been out near his place—which makes the wash pot historic, because John Neely Bryan, founder of Dallas, married a Beeman girl, Margaret, in 1843 (see *Dallas: The Deciding Years* for details). You say you only have a charcoal broiler? Have you looked *really* hard for a pot? Confess: you haven't, have you? (Long pause.) All right. Charcoal broiler.

Don't let the charcoal burn down too far or you can't get that flame-touched finish a beer steak deserves. You might add mesquite chips to the charcoal after it's turned white (see *A Personal Country* for details). I like to let the fire flame up a little—beer steak doesn't really call for a manageable fire, except in the case of Billy Porterfield—then it does.

Now, the most important element in beer steak is not the pot or the fire or, for that matter, the steak. It is the *martini*. My friend Bob Green (no "e") from Albany (Texas, not New York; see *Nine Hundred Miles on the Butterfield Trail* for details) likes a "Crystal Chandelier," and he makes a superb one. But since my heart transplant, I can't do a Crystal Chandelier—or a martini, either (see *Taking Heart* for details). But the martini is important because that's what you sip (not gulp) as you sit out-of-doors by the pot while the beer steak is under way. And there is no hard-and-fast rule about when you start sipping; maybe you'll want to start an hour or so before the steak is put on the grill.

The gin is important, true; but regardless of gin quality, a martini must be made with delicacy. Do not use Tanqueray gin in a martini. Why? It is best sipped straight, maybe with a twist and on the rocks— but in a martini it loses its distinctive "flowers of spring" bouquet. Many people think that if they use Beefeater gin, the martini will take care of itself. Nonsense. My favorite gin is Booth's House of Lords, but it's hard to find. My absolute favorite used to be Bengal gin, which had a semi-enraged tiger (full color) on the label, but it seems to have gone off the market. There was a wonderful gin supposedly distilled on the campus of Oxford University (in England, not Ohio). I once had a lucrative book contract with Oxford University Press, but that heart transplant interfered—and no book. Oxford gin, too, has disappeared.

I keep (kept) a wide-mouth glass Peter Pan peanut butter jar in the freezer for martini preparation, but DO NOT keep your gin in the freezer. Freezing roughens gin. Remember: delicacy. Also, DO NOT use a brutal stirrer; swish the martini and ice around in a circular motion in the wide-mouth Peter Pan peanut butter jar. DO NOT SHAKE. Vermouth? Not too much, but, please, add some. And if you are doing on-the-rocks, don't use the same ice in the glass (chilled) that was used to swish the martini. Once, in Israel, I made martinis using Mount Carmel (local) wine and they drank 'em *very* happily, but Israelis aren't exactly martini experts. My friend Fred Smith likes to put just a drop of Galliano atop a fresh Tequila Sunrise. As I started to say, some people like to put a drop of scotch atop a martini. (John Graves and Dan Jenkins may want ALL scotch.)

I prefer a twist in my martini but certainly will accept an olive . . . and one can acquire a taste for the pearl onion in the martini, but purists insist that's a Gibson. Do as you please. (What's a Crystal Chandelier? By proportion, half gin and half vodka, on the rocks, with three olives.)

Now, about the steak. Can you get Black Angus beef? Try. But be careful. It's delicate, too. Whatever meat, let the wood chips flame up enough to sear the meat, turning very quickly to get both sides. Pour some beer on the chips if they are flaming too much—but don't waste *Dos Equis* or *Samuel Adams* or *Salado Creek* or any beer like that. As the steaks begin to cook, pour a little of the good beer on the steak and stir it around WITH YOUR FINGER. Turn the steak and repeat on the other side. Frequently. Do this until you get what you want: red, rare, or medium rare. It is all right for the cook to slice a small piece from the steak to ascertain its doneness, its texture, or its taste. A slice may be obtained for each of these tests. I like (liked) to cleanse my palate by a sip of beer with and/or between each bite. But take care: I have known Jim Lehrer or Bill Wittliff to consume the entire steak before it ever left the grill and reached the table where the wives were waiting.

The recipe for Kahlúa chicken calls for one cup of Kahlúa, used as a marinade (two to four hours) for separate pieces of chicken—not halves. Either cook in the oven or put on the grill over very low coals until done. Some people like to spread the marinated pieces with smooth peanut butter before cooking. A few prefer chunky peanut butter. Either way, be very careful if preparing the chicken on the charcoal grill. Peanut butter will burn. I don't know what Kahlúa chicken tastes like, with or without peanut butter. I have never made it.

BOOKS

A Personal Country. New York: Knopf, 1969.

Living Texas. Dallas: Hendrick-Long, 1970.

The Last Captive. Austin, Tex.: Encino Press, 1972.

The Santa Claus Bank Robbery. New York: Knopf, 1972.

A Christmas Tree. Austin, Tex.: Encino Press, 1973; miniature ed.,
    Dallas: Somesuch Press, 1980.

Dallas: The Deciding Years. Austin, Tex: Encino Press, 1973.

Views in Texas. Austin, Tex.: Encino Press, 1974.

A Place Called Dallas. Dallas: Dallas County Heritage Society, 1975.

Elephants in Your Mailbox (with Roger Horchow). New York: Times
    Books, 1980.

The Fifty Best Books on Texas. Dallas: Pressworks, 1981.

The Highland Park Woman. Bryan, Tex.: Shearer, 1983.

Dallas, USA. Austin: Texas Monthly Press, 1984.

Texas Sketches. Dallas: Taylor Publishing, 1985.

A Town Called Cedar Springs. Dallas: The Springs, 1985.

It's Been Fun (with J. D. Sandefer, Jr.). Abilene, Tex.: Hardin-Simmons
    University Press, 1986.

Taking Heart. New York: Simon & Schuster, 1990.

Nine Hundred Miles on the Butterfield Trail. Denton: University of
    North Texas Press, 1994.

Joy to the World. Austin: Book Club of Texas, 1995.

Christmas Memories. Denton: University of North Texas Press, 1996.

R. S. Gwynn has published poetry collections and edited numerous literary texts. He teaches creative writing at Lamar University.

R. S. Gwynn

Texas is coming into its own on the national literary scene. Not only do we have award-winning and best-selling mainstream writers, but our regional writers are receiving unqualified (and overdue) praise as well. Book sales are up. Staged readings and review groups no longer are rarities, and writing groups are swelling. The success of the first two annual Texas Book Festivals, spearheaded by Laura Bush and held in Austin in 1996 and 1997, surpassed even the most grandiose expectations.

Having said that, Texas still has its fair share of people who'd just as soon lean against their pickup trucks and tell funny stories as try to decipher poetry. I overheard one ol' boy say, "Half the time, them there poets can't figure what rhymes with what and the rest of the time they write something they theirselves call namby-pamby." (Presumably he meant "iambic pentameter.")

R. S. Gwynn has been publishing poetry for over twenty years and is one of our state's best poets; however, it is not his poetry that is read most widely, but his food reviews. Since 1984, he has been a restaurant reviewer (anonymously, of course) for a major magazine. About that he says, "I don't see any conflict in writing poetry and writing food reviews. I write a lot of poems in fixed forms—sonnets, rondeaus, etc.—because, on one level, I like the challenges of limitation. Writing a 150-word restaurant review is something of a challenge, too. There's a fixed formula to follow and a minimum of information to convey—food, service, ambience, etc.—and I enjoy it. It also pays a lot better than poetry."

And here some of us were thinking that poets spent all their time stretched out beside a pond, staring at the clouds, and sighing. At least one poet gets paid to write about fried chicken. What a deal! Besides, there can't be that much difference between poetry and poultry. The next time I'm leaning against a pickup truck talking to my friends, I'm gonna be sure and bring this up.

R. S. Gwynn's
CRAWFISH ETOUFFEE

Ingredients:

1 cup melted butter
½ cup flour
2 cups chopped onion
1 cup chopped celery
1 cup chopped bell pepper (red and green)
1 clove garlic, minced
Parsley
Bay leaf
Cayenne pepper
Black pepper
Salt
3–4 cups water
2 lbs. peeled crawfish tails
Lemon wedges and chopped green onion tops (for garnish)
Steamed rice

Rondeau Ecrevisses Etouffees

To make it, cher, you got to have some roux.
You brown some butter and flour. Don't overdo
The browning. Add chopped onion, celery,
Bell pepper, garlic. Simmer until they
Are done. Add water, making a thick stew.

Now make it hot. Use pepper, at least two
Kinds, black and red. You want it almost too
Spicy to eat, for that's the Cajun way
    To make it.

Now stir your fresh-peeled crawfish tails into
That roux and simmer till they're heated through.
Add salt and pepper, parsley, and a bay
Leaf while they cook. This crawfish etouffee
Is good with rice. I hope this has helped you
  To make it.

BOOKS
The Drive-In. Columbia: University of Missouri Press, 1986.

EDITED BOOKS
Dictionary of Literary Biography. Vol. 105, *American Poets Since World War II, Second Series*. Columbia, Mo.: Bruccoli Clark Layman, 1991.
Dictionary of Literary Biography. Vol. 120, *American Poets Since World War II, Third Series*. Columbia, Mo.: Bruccoli Clark Layman, 1992.
Drama: A HarperCollins Pocket Anthology. New York: HarperCollins, 1993.
Fiction: A HarperCollins Pocket Anthology. New York: HarperCollins, 1993.
Poetry: A HarperCollins Pocket Anthology. New York: HarperCollins, 1993.
The Advocates of Poetry: American Poet-Critics of the Modern Era. Fayetteville: University of Arkansas Press, 1996.

POETRY CHAPBOOKS
Bearing and Distance. New Braunfels, Tex.: Cedar Rock, 1977.
The Narcissiad. New Braunfels, Tex.: Cedar Rock, 1981.
Body Bags. In *Texas Poets in Concert: A Quartet*. Denton: University of North Texas Press, 1990.
The Area Code of God. Westchester, N.Y.: Aralia, 1994.
No Word of Farewell. Westchester, N.Y.: Pikeman, 1996.

Stephen Harrigan is a former senior editor of Texas Monthly *magazine. He is best known for his essay collections, but also writes screenplays and fiction.*

Stephen Harrigan

When I commented to Stephen Harrigan that I thought many writers were self-absorbed and egotistical, he corrected me. "No, you're wrong," he said. "Not *many* writers. *All* writers." This seemed an odd statement coming from one of the least self-impressed men that I had ever met. When I acted surprised, he explained that when writers are first starting out, they have to shout to be heard above the din. Consequently, they affect bravado and often try too hard. He claims that he had that tendency early on but has come to believe that being perceived as genuine and as a quiet authority is more desirable than being considered clever. (For the record, I have been reading Steve's work since his years at *Texas Monthly* and disagree with the part about him being a chest-beater, ever.)

This unpretentiousness spills over into his attitude toward his craft. For instance, I have talked to a number of authors who have a set routine when it's time to write. A common requirement is that they must be alone at their desk—no noise or interruptions permitted—because, after all, an artist is at work. Not Steve. He welcomes the phone ringing or an interruption from his wife or one of his three daughters and finds excuses to leave his garage–converted office to go rummage around in the kitchen. Although he takes it seriously, writing is, simply put, what he does for a living. He places neither himself nor his profession in an exalted spot.

Finally, he's not snobby about doing all types of writing. There are the essays, of course, but he has also written other types of nonfiction, screenplays, and novels. He even claims that nonfiction is the most difficult. I thought that was a very nice thing to say to someone who has been told—often subtly, but not always—that she is not a real writer, because she writes only nonfiction. Just an awfully nice thing to say.

Stephen Harrigan's
PIE CRUST COOKIES

My tastes are primitive. I like big, yeasty hunks of things. My all-time favorite food? The unparalleled hot rolls served by Underwood's barbecue cafeteria in Brownwood, Texas. The name Harrigan is about as Irish as you can get, but my genetic material seems to come entirely from the Czech side of the family; hence my body's slow, methodical metabolism and its shrieking demand for gluten in any form.

Which brings us to pie crust, which is so basic a food it belongs on the Periodic Table of the Elements. If you're a doughboy like me, pie is merely an excuse to consume pie crust. It always aggravates me to watch my wife, Sue Ellen, eat a piece of pumpkin pie. Bite by bite, she delicately scoops out the odious filling, never deigning to eat the crust itself, which she seems to regard as some sort of disposable plate.

The irony is that she makes great pie crust herself (see recipe below). The pie-baking spirit moves her every six months or so, and on those occasions I seize the opportunity to practice my lonely specialty, Pie Crust Cookies. While Sue Ellen is fluting the edges of the dough in the pie plates, I am gathering up the scraps. In my heedless youth I used to just pile wads of pie crust on a cookie sheet and throw it into the oven, but now that I'm older and more concerned with presentation, I roll out the dough and cut it into various shapes using a drawerful of old cookie cutters. The ideal thickness is a quarter of an inch; any less than that and the cookies won't hold their shape. Mostly for form's sake, I sprinkle them with cinnamon and sugar; but the truth is, the less they taste like anything, the more I like them.

I think Sue Ellen cooks her pies at 350 degrees, so that must be the oven temperature when I put them in. They burn fast if you don't watch them. When they're done, they should be deep brown and as dried out as old parchment. They should not be allowed to cool, but should burn your tongue when you eat them. They're probably good served with milk, if you like milk. I don't.

Sue Ellen and our three daughters regard Pie Crust Cookies with varying degrees of indifference. But we have two dogs, and though they were not enthusiastic at first, they have managed to acquire the taste.

Sue Ellen's Pie Crust

(loosely adapted from Linda West Eckhardt's *The Only Texas Cookbook*)

Put three cups sifted flour, one and one-fourth cups Crisco, and a pinch of salt into a bowl. Work it with your hands until it becomes crumbly. Beat together one egg, five and a half tbs. water, and one tsp. vinegar. Pour into the flour and mix. Divide the dough into two balls and roll out. Makes two pie crusts.

BOOKS

Aransas. New York: Knopf, 1980.

Jacob's Well. New York: Simon & Schuster, 1984.

A Natural State. Austin: Texas Monthly Press, 1988; paperback, Austin: University of Texas Press, 1994.

Water and Light. Boston: Houghton Mifflin, 1992.

Comanche Midnight. Austin: University of Texas Press, 1994.

The Gates of the Alamo. New York: Knopf, forthcoming.

Rolando Hinojosa-Smith

Rolando Hinojosa-Smith is internationally
recognized for his award-winning
contributions to Texas-Mexican literature.
He is the Ellen Clayton Garwood Professor of
English at the University of Texas at Austin.

Rolando Hinojosa-Smith

Collecting recipes for this book required nothing less than a good, solid sales job. I had to convince authors—most of whom didn't know me from Adam—that they should participate in a writing project for little more than a free copy of the book. Furthermore, the project probably seemed like something the women down at the Baptist church would be up to. In short, hokey. Approaching the authors took a lot of nerve, particularly when the author was someone like Rolando Hinojosa-Smith.

Here's a guy who has published a whole slew of books, is the Ellen Clayton Garwood Professor of English at the University of Texas, and even serves as the University's marshal—you know, that real distinguished-looking person leading the graduation ceremony wearing a cap and gown and a drapey thing around the neck. And, here's a guy who is so important not only in Texan but in *world* literature that treatises about his work have been written in France, Germany, Italy, the Netherlands, Spain, Sweden, and the United States. There's even a full-length book by Joyce Glover Lee entitled *Rolando Hinojosa and the American Dream* (Denton: University of North Texas Press, 1997). Yet here I go, asking the guy to stop what he's doing and write down a *recipe*, for crying out loud.

Dr. Hinojosa-Smith not only stopped what he was doing and wrote down a recipe, but he also congratulated me on the cleverness of the concept and the title. After we played phone tag for a couple of days, he apologized for being so hard to catch, as if it were my time instead of his that was at a premium. When we finally did have a chance to talk, he patiently answered all my questions, made me laugh, and with the graciousness of a consummate gentleman, thanked me for inviting him to contribute to this book. What a great guy!

Rolando Hinojosa-Smith's
SOPA DE ARROZ Y SOPA DE FIDEO

This paragraph opens with a small complaint against the uninhibited assertiveness often manifested when speaking of food in general. Language a bit pedantic that, but it may serve to get someone's attention. It's a cry for the acceptance of variants.

One cannot account for variants. For example, years ago, I once ordered an enchilada in Santa Fe. I didn't recognize it, particularly when there I saw a fried egg on top of what looked like a hamburger patty. Well, the patty turned out to be a flattened blue corn tortilla, the first I'd ever seen, and thus my ignorance. Added to which, the fried egg rested on red chile sauce, a New Mexican treat.

The taste was all right, but I missed the rolled tortillas, the cheese, the sauce, the black pepper and cumin—in short, the Tex-Mex food I'd become used to eating from Dalhart to Brownsville, from Houston to El Paso.

For my part, the enchiladas I ate for the first seventeen years of my life consisted of tortillas doused in a poblano pepper sauce. The tortillas were then stuffed with white (usually goat) cheese and onions, they were then rolled, and then shredded and sprinkled liberally throughout with additional cheese.

Quite simple, really, but tasty. Different, too, from the usual enchiladas one is served at restaurants. Not better, as I said, merely different.

The word *enchilada* has an interesting etymology. The word is both an adjective and a noun, depending on its use. The *ada* ending is a singular feminine modifying the adjective *tortilla*. *Tortilla* is also used as a noun since it's an object. The suffix *en* is usually the equivalent of the English *in,* as in making something or inserting something. Here, though, it also stands for *to.* For example, the noun *silla,* chair, is also the Spanish noun for saddle. So, to put a saddle on an animal is *en*sillar; and to put, add, douse, etc., chile on a tortilla is to *enchilar* the tortilla. You'll note that since we've borrowed the word *tortilla* from the Spanish, the word isn't either underlined or in italics. The same goes for salsa, taco, and other Mexican-Spanish language borrowings.

Incidentally, the Mexican tortilla is different from the Spanish tortilla. The name in both cases derives from the word *torta,* but the meanings are not the same. The Spanish tortilla usually consists of eggs, potatoes, and onions which are fried in a round pan, the shape creating a resemblance to the Mexican tortilla. There the resemblance ends, however. As can be seen, the Spanish tortilla promises the eater a healthy jolt of cholesterol, as well as calories.

But back to variants. The ingredients I was taught at home to use for Arroz Norteño and Fideo del Norte (I make no claim as to why they are so called) are:

Long or short-grained rice, 1 cup
Half a medium can of unpeeled tomatoes
Half a teaspoon of cumin
Half a teaspoon of coarse black pepper
Three-quarters teaspoon salt
One small onion
One-half small green bell pepper
Four-and-a-half cups of water

Steps:

Use a non-stick fry pan, thus no oil, shortening, or Pam. Otherwise, a light film of oil, shortening, etc., will do.

Set the skillet at 375 degrees.

Mince the onion and green pepper and set aside.

Crush, do not frappé, the tomatoes; use half of the juice from the can.

Toast the rice; remember, add no oil.

When toasted, add the tomato and the juice, the water, onion, bell pepper, and spices.

Cover and cook for 20–22 minutes.

Do not stir rice at any time during cooking.

The *fideo* recipe is the same but with an additional quarter-cup of water. You'll discover that the taste is quite different.

The preferred *fideo* brand, *Quantity and Quality,* has been around for half a century and comes in a red-orange and yellow box. If unavailable, you may use the thinnest vermicelli, broken in half. Q and Q offers a variant, and the word *fideo* is printed on the box.

There is a pleasant variant for both the arroz and the fideo, as you will see later on.

Aside from the dish, the additional water also produces the *caldo de fideo,* which may be used as a starter for dinner. The caldo is a pleasant, tangy soup. (*Sopa* is not a cognate for *soup.*)

Variants: During Lent, a small minced potato may be added to the arroz and the fideo. This, though, will call for an additional quarter-teaspoon of salt and a quarter-cup of water, since the potato absorbs some of both. One may substitute dried shrimp for the potato, and that, too, produces a tasty dish.

You may have noticed that Mexican restaurants serve the salsa separately. We use the salsa as a dip for the ever-present tortilla chips. While Mexicans do eat tortillas con chile, the restaurant chips are an American addition to Mexican cuisine. Hollywood cartoons and such notwithstanding, salsa is always served separately for the practical reason that each person has a personal tolerance for hot sauce.

New Mexico and parts of Arizona are the exceptions, but don't ask me why. The custom of using hot peppers certainly couldn't have come from Spain, where garlic, cumin, and other spices are the hottest condiments used. The Spaniards, by the way, use the term *ají* for chile.

A few last words. I've no idea why the *New Yorker* advertisement refers to Habanero peppers as Habañero; ignorance may be a candidate for that answer. Not to be too harsh on our fellow citizens from Up North, however, some of us Texans sometimes add an extra "e" to *jalapeño* and call it *jalapeeno.*

In passing. A close friend told me that Texas A&M University was developing, or had developed, a jalapeño that wasn't hot to the taste. If this isn't another Aggie joke, then the question is: why would they?

Shortcuts: I've found that by mixing a can of frijoles refritos and a can of whole pinto beans, then mashing them, they take on a homemade quality.

Every region and many households, then, use variants of variants, but this is what adds to the spice of life's pleasure in cooking and eating. I would suggest that when planning to cook either the arroz or the fideo, for example, fool around, be creative—after all, there's no patent on any of this.

BOOKS

Estampas del Valle. Berkeley, Calif.: Quinto Sol, 1973.

Klail City y Sus Alredeores. Havana: Casa de las Américas, 1976.

Korean Love Songs. Berkeley, Calif.: Justa Publications, 1978.

Mi Querido Rafa. Houston: Arte Público Press, 1981.

Rites and Witnesses. Houston: Arte Público Press, 1982.

The Valley. Ypsilanti, Mich.: Bilingual Press, 1983.

Dear Rafe. Houston: Arte Público Press, 1985.

Partners in Crime. Houston: Arte Público Press, 1985.

Claros Varones de Belken. Tempe, Ariz.: Editorial Bilingue, 1986.

Klail City. Houston: Arte Público Press, 1987.

Becky and Her Friends. Houston: Arte Público Press, 1990.

Los Amigos de Becky. Houston: Arte Público Press, 1991.

The Useless Servants. Houston: Arte Público Press, 1993.

*Molly Ivins is a well known Texas
journalist and political commentator.
She has written for numerous national
magazines and newspapers.*

Molly Ivins

By her own estimation, Molly Ivins is not cute. In her book, *Molly Ivins Can't Say That, Can She?* (New York: Random House, 1991), she says, "I should confess that I've always been more of an observer than a participant in Texas Womanhood: the spirit was willing but I was declared ineligible on grounds of size early. You can't be six feet tall and cute, both." If you follow her political columns or have heard her speak, you also know that she is not one to bat her eyelashes coyly. In fact, she never blinks first. This is advantageous, though, since she is of a mind to go turning over big, flat rocks. Being winsome and demure is a sure way to lose a stare-down with the slithery, fanged creatures that hide under big, flat rocks. All the same, at an Austin fund-raiser for Philosophers Rock, Ms. Ivins showed that she has more to her character than meets the eye—or ear.

You will recall that Philosophers Rock is a commissioned statue of Texas's literary legends J. Frank Dobie, folklorist; Walter Prescott Webb, historian; and Roy Bedichek, naturalist. It is at the entrance to Barton Springs in Austin. You also will recall that funds for its construction were donated.

To raise some of this money, Ms. Ivins was invited to take part in a reading called "Voices of Texas: A Celebration of Lone Star Literature." A capacity crowd gathered at La Zona Rosa, ate barbecue, and settled back to hear readings by Liz Carpenter, Kinky Friedman, John Graves, and Ms. Ivins. When time came for her to read, Ms. Ivins was nowhere to be found. Emcee Billy Porterfield made a few Billy Porterfieldian remarks to kill time and then forged on with the program. A while later, Ms. Ivins showed up, straight from the airport, breathless and disheveled.

The crowd, by now restless and a bit fanged, applauded only half-heartedly when she stepped up to the microphone; however, instead of launching into one of her notoriously funny and profane diatribes, she surprised everyone by offering a heartfelt apology for being late. She then tucked her hands behind her back and, without reading from a prepared text, delivered a moving oration. I can't even remember who or what it was she talked about. Someone she admired, maybe? A friend of hers? It doesn't matter, because the results were magical. The crowd grew quiet and leaned forward in their folding chairs, feasting on her outstretched words. And Ms. Ivins, who only minutes before had looked disheveled, transformed into a captivating woman, all six feet of her. When she finished speaking, she received the only standing ovation of the day.

Cute women, eat your hearts out.

Molly Ivins's

COMPOSED SALAD OF SAUSAGE AND ORZO WITH FRESH PEAS AND MIXED GREENS

2 cups orzo (about 12 ounces)
2 cups shelled fresh green peas (about 2 lbs. in the pod)
1 large garlic clove, minced
$\frac{1}{2}$ cup pine nuts
12 sweet Italian sausages (about 2 lbs.)
$\frac{1}{4}$ cup dry red wine
$\frac{1}{2}$ cup chopped scallions
2 tbs. Dijon-style mustard
$1\frac{1}{2}$ tsp. salt
$\frac{1}{2}$ cup plus $1\frac{1}{2}$ tbs. olive oil
4 bunches of lamb's lettuce (mache), about $\frac{1}{2}$ lb.
8 small radicchio leaves, torn into pieces
2 tbs. red wine vinegar
1 tbs. mayonnaise
$\frac{3}{4}$ tsp. freshly ground pepper
2 Belgian endives, cut into thin strips
2 tsp. fresh lemon juice

1. Preheat the oven to 375 degrees. Bring a large saucepan of salted water to a boil over high heat. Stir in the orzo and cook until the pasta is tender but still firm, about 10 minutes. Drain and rinse under cold running water; drain well.

2. Scatter the pine nuts over a small baking sheet and toast in the oven until golden brown, about 10 minutes (Note: 10 minutes on *heavy* sheet; on a thin cookie sheet they burn easily).

3. Steam the peas over boiling water until just tender, about 6 minutes. Rinse under cold running water; drain well.

4. Prick the sausages all over with a fork. In a large skillet, cook the sausages over moderately high heat (medium), turning, until browned, about 10 minutes. Pour off all of the fat. Add the garlic and wine to the skillet. Reduce the heat to low, cover and simmer for 20 minutes. Remove the sausages. Degrease the juice in the pan and set aside.

5. In large bowl, mix together the orzo, peas, pine nuts, and scallions. In a small bowl, whisk together the vinegar, mustard, mayonnaise, 1 teaspoon of the salt, and $\frac{1}{2}$ teaspoon of the pepper. Gradually whisk in $\frac{1}{3}$ cup of the olive oil and the reserved pan juices, until well blended. Add to the orzo and stir to coat.

6. In a large bowl, toss together the lamb's lettuce, Belgian endives, and radicchio. Drizzle the lemon juice and the remaining $1\frac{1}{2}$ tablespoons olive oil over the salad. Season with the remaining $\frac{1}{2}$ teaspoon salt and $\frac{1}{4}$ teaspoon pepper and toss.

7. Place a portion of the greens on each plate, top with a portion of the orzo mixture and arrange 2 sausages, sliced if you like, over the top of the salads.

Note: This recipe was given to Molly Ivins by Jocelyn Gray, who noted, "This is a totally flexible recipe—I've never done the sausage; if you don't like peas, use something(s) else; and of course you don't have to use designer lettuce."

BOOKS

Molly Ivins Can't Say That, Can She? New York: Random House, 1991.
Nothin' but Good Times Ahead. New York: Random House, 1993.
You Got to Dance with Them What Brung You: Politics in the Clinton Years. New York: Random House, 1998.

Elmer Kelton is an award-winning novelist and journalist who has been honored for life-time achievement by Western Writers of America, the Texas Institute of Letters, and the Western Literature Association.

Elmer Kelton

Except for my first two years of medical school, when I was by myself in Dallas, I have spent my whole life living with first one and then another West Texas man. Born daughter to one and later becoming wife to another, I figure I have as fair a view as the next person about what distinguishes West Texas men from those of other places.

Before he utters a drawl-drenched word and leaves no doubt about his upbringing, you know that Elmer Kelton is a West Texas man. His gait is deliberate, with footfall as quiet as dust settling. His big hands are completely still when he is talking and when he is listening also, which, in social situations, he does more of than talking. His facial expressions also are spare, with a smile that, although kind and genuine, emerges and fades slowly. When women are around, the economy of his movements and words is particularly apparent and verges on friendly cautiousness.

To the casual eye, the West Texas landscape is unassuming; however, the weather and the country can be harsh, especially to those who work the hardest. Elmer Kelton has known men and women who have been brought to their knees by this country. His reverence for those people and his fierce love for this country—this Elmer Kelton country—form the quiet center that gives rise to his unmatched books.

Elmer Kelton's

LINZERTORTE

First of all, let me say that I am not a cook. I proved that more than fifty years ago during a couple of summers when I was in high school. My father had a ranch leased west of Crane, Texas, and after school was out, he sent me there to watch over it while the regular caretaker took the summer off. My three younger brothers would come to help me, one at a time. It was strictly a batching outfit, and I did the cooking.

My brothers could only stay about a week at a time before they starved out. They rotated, under protest, one week with me and two weeks at home to recuperate on Mother's cooking.

The years have not improved my performance in the kitchen. When I boil water, it smells scorched. But my Austrian-born wife Ann is a good cook. The most popular recipe she has is for a type of Austrian cake known as the Linzertorte, named for its city of origin, Linz, where I was stationed a few months in 1946 as a go-fer, a lowly private first class. She has made a few minor modifications from the original, for instance using pecans rather than almonds or walnuts, because pecans are much more readily available in Texas. We grow our own.

The torte is a little tricky to make, and some people have trouble getting the proper consistency in the dough the first time they try. It must be kneaded, preferably by hand, until it is soft and sticks together well. People sometimes are tempted to add extra flour. That makes the dough too dry. It crumbles and will not stick together.

The cakes keep well if wrapped in airtight foil or plastic, and they also freeze well. Ann usually makes up a large number before Christmas. Any leftover tortes are put in the freezer, and we have thawed them as late as the following summer with good results.

A word of caution: don't make the slices too large. This is definitely *not* a low-cal dessert.

Ingredients:
2 cups (very fine) ground pecans (or almonds or walnuts)
2 sticks butter
2⅔ cups flour
1⅓ cups sugar
1 whole egg and 2 yolks
1 tsp. cloves
1 tsp. cinnamon
2 tsp. ground lemon peel
1 cup plum jam

Steps:

Mix in a large bowl.

Cut butter into the flour as for a pie crust, then mix sugar, pecans, spices, and lemon peel in with the flour. Make a well in the center, then add the eggs. Mix thoroughly until it sticks together, then place on dough board and keep working it until smooth. (The dough will be sticky, but don't add flour.)

Press two-thirds of the dough into a 9-inch spring-form cake pan (don't grease pan). Spread 1 cup jam evenly over top, ½ inch from side of pan.

Roll remaining dough pencil-thick and arrange it around side of pan and criss-cross over top of jam.

For cake, bake one hour at 350 degrees.

For cookies, press dough into small balls and press center with ⅛ teaspoon to make indentation, put jam inside indentation. Bake 15 minutes at 350 degrees.

BOOKS

Hot Iron. New York: Ballantine, 1955.
The Texas Rifles. New York: Ballantine, 1960.

Massacre at Goliad. New York: Ballantine, 1965.
The Day the Cowboys Quit. Garden City, N.Y.: Doubleday, 1971.
The Time It Never Rained. Garden City, N.Y.: Doubleday, 1973.
Manhunters. New York: Ballantine, 1974.
Joe Pepper. Garden City, N.Y.: Doubleday, 1975.
Long Way to Texas. Garden City, N.Y.: Doubleday, 1976.
The Good Old Boys. Garden City, N.Y.: Doubleday, 1978.
The Wolf and the Buffalo. Garden City, N.Y.: Doubleday, 1980.
Eyes of the Hawk. Garden City, N.Y.: Doubleday, 1981.
Stand Proud. Garden City, N.Y.: Doubleday, 1984.
The Man Who Rode Midnight. Garden City, N.Y.: Doubleday, 1987.
Honor at Daybreak. Garden City, N.Y.: Doubleday, 1991.
Slaughter. Garden City, N.Y.: Doubleday, 1992.
The Far Canyon. Garden City, N.Y.: Doubleday, 1994.
My Kind of Heroes. Austin, Tex.: Statehouse Press, 1995.
The Pumpkin Rollers. New York: Forge Books, 1996.
Cloudy in the West. New York: Forge Books, 1997.
And others

Larry L. King is a winner of the Helen Hayes Award and the Mary Goldwater Award. He has received critical acclaim for many of his plays, the most famous of which is The Best Little Whorehouse in Texas.

Larry L. King

While compiling this book, I had the chance to talk with many Texas authors. One of the recurring subjects was Larry L. King. It seems that nearly everyone who has spent a measure with the written words of Texans has a Larry King anecdote to share. Some are printable. Some—okay, most—aren't. In the latter category is a story about what Mr. King threatened to do to a man who (unfavorably) reviewed one of his books in a Dallas newspaper. Maybe someone needs to tell Mr. King that a bad book review sells as many books as a good book review. After hearing some of the Larry King stories, let me assure you that I won't be the one to tell him. In fact, I vote we get Billy Porterfield to do it. Mr. Porterfield has a long-standing gentleman's agreement with Mr. King: If Mr. King lifts a finger against Mr. Porterfield, the latter will summarily shoot the former.

So there.

When Mr. King read this piece, he wrote me the following note (edited for decency's sake): "Porterfield is so old and blind I could kill him with a popgun. Maybe a slingshot."

Mr. Porterfield's response (edited for decency's sake) is as follows: "I'm not saying this out of a wimp's fawning tergiversation or fear, even if Larry Leo is a foot taller than me in all the ways warriors and writers are judged by Barnum's public. Hell, all are taller'n me, even my youngest woman child. As to Master King's repute, I'm simply stating a fact that has become legend. King doesn't live an idle life or make idle threats. After all, he was, among other things, Satan's older brother and Tom Sawyer's shadow before he became LBJ's hack. If he had never written a word, he would still be legend for the heft of his basso profundo roar and the hum in his haunch as he springs to the kill."

Speaking of killing (and being killed), I believe I'll quietly back away from this showdown before it progresses to six-shooters—or worse. Billy Porterfield did, after all, accuse me of trying to start a pissing contest between two prostatic old men.

Larry L. King
DR. KING'S ASIAN FLU HOT LIQUID LIFE-SAVER

Put on old bathrobe and work up sweat by running up and down stairs while thinking of the money you owe and how many years you may be required to serve should the I.R.S. audit your most recent tax returns.

Once sweating good, prepare Loved Ones for what may soon follow by claiming to have a bad case of Asian Flu and that The Only Cure Known To Medical Science is Dr. King's Asian Flu Hot Liquid Life-saver. Give Loved Ones as much money as you can afford and suggest they absent themselves for twenty-four hours, on account of you will be contagious for that duration. Lock and bar all doors and windows once they disappear. Do not let anyone in, even should they shout through megaphones.

Quickly pour into strong two-handled pot—the bigger the better—equal measures of vodka, scotch, bourbon, beer, gin, tequila, rum, and other handy adult potables. Hum and grin as you add $\frac{1}{2}$ pinch of salt, full pinch of chili powder, one crushed-to-smithereens jalapeño pepper and $\frac{1}{3}$ diced onion. Let simmer on burner at "low heat" until fumes make your eyes smart, being careful—always—not to contact burner with any part of old bathrobe. Hide car keys, disconnect telephone, stow all stepladders and put karaoke tape on recorder. Take two aspirins, then commence drinking Hot Liquid Life-saver the instant ingredients won't blister tongue. Serves one. All night long.

BOOKS

Confessions of a White Racist. New York: Viking, 1971.

Of Outlaws, Con Men, Whores, Politicians, and Other Artists. New York: Viking, 1980.

The Whorehouse Papers. New York: Viking, 1982

Warning: Writer at Work. Fort Worth: Texas Christian University Press, 1985.

True Facts, Tall Tales, Pure Fiction. Austin: University of Texas Press, 1997.

And others

STAGE PLAYS

The Best Little Whorehouse in Texas (with Peter Masterson and Carol Hall). 1978.

The Kingfish (with Ben Z. Grant). 1979.

The Night Hank Williams Died. 1988.

The Dead Presidents' Club. 1996.

And others

James Ward Lee

James Ward Lee, well-known for his
humorous speeches and articles, has also published widely in folklore and the literatures of
Britain, America, and Texas.

James Ward Lee

James Ward Lee and Robert Flynn co-teach a seminar on writing humor. This is for good reason, since both of them are very funny men. In their more polite public moments and in print, each of them nods to the other as being the funniest writer in Texas; however, if you get either of them off to the side, they both shed their modesty and declare straight-faced that they are funnier than the other. Whether he, in fact, occupies first or second place, James Ward Lee is a funny, funny man. His sidelong opinions and his anecdotes are funny enough, but his telling of them in his native Alabama tongue, laced with colloquialisms, makes him sidesplittingly funny. For this reason, picking out a single story to tell about him is like trying to decide on which morsel to take from a Lamme's Candy gift basket—each of the choices is so enticing that you are paralyzed with indecision. So, instead of trying to settle on one story about James Ward Lee, I will instead tell a story about his granddaughter.

One Sunday morning, the four-year-old's mother reasoned with her, "You have two choices. If you promise to sit still, you can go to Big Church with me. If you want to, though, you can stay in the nursery and play with the other children. It's your choice."

The little girl thought for a moment and replied, "No, Mommy, those are *your* choices. My choice is that we go home."

There is little doubt about which branch of the family tree gave rise to that twig.

James Ward Lee

HIS RECIPES

Here is a word of warning: If you cook by the local church cookbook—and I hope you don't—you might as well stop now. You won't find "a can of mushroom soup" or "a ten-ounce package of frozen broccoli" mentioned here. As a matter of fact, you may have to kill a hog. But that is fine with me; as Mr. Bob Dole used to say, "Whatever."

So you've been warned.

O.K., here are three of the best recipes in the world.

Neckbones and Liver

Kill a hog and take the liver on in the house. Let somebody else worry about butchering and rendering lard and making cracklin's and cleaning out the chitlin's. You have better things to do. Killing a hog may not be necessary if you live where the grocery store sells pork liver. I used to, but then they took to selling tofu and radiche and foreign stuff, so pork liver disappeared from the meat case. They still have plenty of calf's liver—probably old cow's liver—but it is not at all like pork liver. I mean, a cow's liver works the same way in the cow that a hog liver works in a hog, but forget that.

Now throw a pound or two of liver in a great big stewer full of water and commence to boil it. This is going to take you about two hours, and you are going to have to keep skimming the foam off the top of the water. Don't ask me what the foam is! I know, but I am not going into that.

After two hours of steady boiling, add an onion or two, a teaspoon or two of salt, some pepper, and a pound or two of neckbones. I am lying about the neckbones. I hardly ever see neckbones in the butcher case, but since you are killing a hog anyway. . . . The thing is, neckbones are not nearly as good as what the butchers call "country backbone." But if you are too poor to buy backbone, neckbones will do. That's how this dish got started. Among poor people. Now you have one hour more to cook this most wonderful of country dishes. Pour some of the juice over cornbread—if you don't already know how to make cornbread, go back to your Junior League cookbook and leave me alone. Now take the liver and mash it up with the juicy cornbread.

The liver is now almost exactly the same consistency as the cornbread. Now don't be comparing this liver to calf liver; they are nothing alike.

Note: When I say some salt and pepper, that's as far as I am going. If you can't cook and taste as you go along, you are not going to be able to fix any of these dishes anyway. Get you a Martha Stewart cookbook and turn fancy.

1 lb. pork liver
1 lb. neckbones
1 large onion
some salt
some pepper

Fried Corn

Now fried corn may look a little like that dreadful creamed corn you see in the cafeteria line or in cans in the store, but don't be misled. Creamed corn is not fit to eat, but fried corn is the best summer dish in the world. Take five or six ears of fresh corn—preferably sweet corn but any kind will work, as you will see if you keep on reading. We used to call these young fresh ears of corn "roast nears," which I think was a fast way of saying "roasting ears," though no country people I knew ever roasted one.

Anyway, back to business: take five or six—or eight—ears of corn, shuck them, hold them under running water while you take a brush and get *every last* bit of corn silk out of the rows of corn. About this time, fry four or five rashers of bacon (that is "strips" to city folks) in an iron skillet and set the bacon aside while you cut the corn off the ears. Wait! Not so fast here. Don't just cut the kernels off the cob. First, take a sharp knife and cut a line (longways) down each row of kernels. Now, rotate the corn while you shave—I said *shave*—the corn off the cob—again from top to bottom—into a big bowl. If you do this right, it will take you seven or eight turns of the corn cob to get the corn sliced off right. O.K. now, take your knife and, holding it perpendicular to the cob, scrape the last of the milk from the cob. Do this to all six or eight ears of corn or until you are worn to a nub—like the corncobs now are. Nubs, I mean.

Now rest a few minutes. Put all the corn in the bacon grease and turn up the fire. Cut up an onion—I mean cut it fine—and throw it in with the corn and grease. Crumble the bacon into the corn and cook away. You are going to need a little salt, a little pepper, a little water or milk (or both) and some sugar if the corn is not naturally sweet. (See I told you it didn't *have* to be sweet; you can fix that.) Now stir and cook, stir and cook, stir and cook, adding whatever is necessary to keep it from drying out. I never said this dish was easy. If you fix this dish and fix it right, you are going to agree with everybody else that old James Ward is the finest country cook in Texas—maybe in the whole South.

8 ears of fresh unshucked corn
5 strips of bacon
1 small onion
some water
some milk
some salt
some pepper
some sugar (maybe)

Collards and Rape

First, go to the seed store and buy some rape seed and plant them. You are never going to find rape in the store. (Rape is a kind of greens; they grow it all over Europe to get rape-seed oil. I don't know—and don't care—what rape-seed oil is for. I am a cook, not a botanist.) O.K., time passes, the rape will get grown about the same time the collards do. (Did I forget to mention that you need to plant some collards, too?) Well, if you do this—and I know you are not going to—you are ready to make the world's best greens. O.K. You don't want to fool with planting rape? Here is what you do. Buy two bunches of collards at the store and one bunch of mustard greens. Wash these greens eternally—or until you get all the grit out. Then get the big veins out of the collards and cut—or tear—the collards and rape (mustard greens) up. (Here is some news. You have always heard that collards are bitter until after the first frost, right? Well, my Aunt Rene got around that: she put the torn up collards in the freezer just long enough to "frost" them good, and "Voilá!" as we used to say back in Alabama, all the bitterness was gone.)

All right. Throw the collards and the rape (or mustard greens) into a pot and put a cup or two of water in the pot. Fire it up and then throw a piece of fat meat (hog jowl, fatback, sow belly, salt pork, or whatever you call it) into the pot. You'll need a piece about as big as a package of Pall Malls. Now some salt and pepper and—do I need to say that?—some sugar. Cook away. You'll know when it is done. Just keep tasting it. You might even put a spoon or two of vinegar into the pot. To quote Mr. Dole again, "Whatever."

    2 bunches of collards
    1 bunch of mustard greens (rape if you can get it)
    1 chunk of fat meat
    some water
    some pepper
    some salt
    some vinegar (if you want to)
    some sugar (if you have to)

Now, put all three of these dishes on the table with a wheel of cornbread—even Martha Stewart probably knows how to cook cornbread—and some iced tea. The only other things you may need are pepper sauce and a few slices of sweet onion. (Hot onions can be sweetened by soaking them in iced water for a long time. See, I know everything!)

If you are on a diet, forget this. My local grocery store still sells tofu and kumquats and stuff, and yours probably does, too.

BOOKS

William Humphrey. Austin, Tex.: Steck-Vaughan, 1967.
John Braine. New York: Twayne, 1968.
Classics of Texas Fiction. Dallas: E-Heart, 1986.
Texas, My Texas. Denton: University of North Texas Press, 1992.

Prudence Mackintosh is a reflective and humorous essayist who writes about her life as a Texas woman and mother. Although she is best known for her work at Texas Monthly, *she has written for many other magazines and newspapers.*

Prudence Mackintosh

Keeping the other joys and demands of life in perspective sometimes is hard when you're a writer. Writing is such a kick that you sometimes wish that you could push the "Pause" button on life's remote control and just keep on writing. Spouses and children may not understand this. After all, even if you *are* in the throes of the final draft of what you know, just know, is the next blockbuster, your family members still want supper on the table and clean underwear in the drawer and toothpaste in the bathroom when they go to brush their teeth. They also want you to listen with your whole brain when they tell you about their own victories and disappointments.

I witnessed something that makes me think that Prudence Mackintosh has struck a healthy balance between her writing life and her family life. It was a muggy Saturday afternoon in the book-signing tent at the first annual Texas Book Festival in Austin. Hundreds of book buyers were standing in cheerful, jagged lines to have their books inscribed by the Texas authors sitting at the signing tables. Because she is so funny and friendly, and because she has such a terrific East Texas accent, we who were waiting in Ms. Mackintosh's line looked like we were in an E. F. Hutton commercial—all leaning forward to hear what she was saying. Standing off to the side of the line were two men, not bending forward but simply watching Ms. Mackintosh. Occasionally they would mumble something to each other, but they continued to watch her, smiling, clearly taken with Ms. Mackintosh. Finally, the younger of the two said, loud enough for all us E. F. Hutton-types to hear, "Dad, do you think Mom might be getting thirsty?" The younger man then hurried away on his important mission, leaving the older one to watch over the woman they both love.

Prudence Mackintosh's
CALVES' LIVER
(DISGUISED AS CHICKEN FRIED STEAK)

Looking back at my first book, *Thundering Sneakers,* I seem to have spent an inordinate amount of time trying to improve my kids' taste in food—in everything. In a chapter called "Food for Thought," I lamented to a priest, "You will know my sons at the communion rail, Father. They will be the ones who ask, before receiving the wafer, "Does it have nuts?"

My husband thinks I am a terrific cook, but I think my sons still prefer Domino's pizza to anything I prepare. I'm not surprised that they never liked calves' liver. Most people don't. My husband John and I were brought up in the fifties, however, when liver was still good for you and parents did not encourage children to become food critics. Perhaps for nostalgia's sake, I occasionally tried to inflict it on our children, disguised as chicken fried steak with this recipe.

   1 lb. calves liver
   2 egg yolks
   3 tbs. butter
   2 tsp. vinegar
   2 tsp. Worcestershire sauce
   $1\frac{1}{2}$ tsp. salt
   1 tsp. dry mustard
   $\frac{1}{2}$ tsp. pepper
   $\frac{1}{4}$ tsp. paprika
   $\frac{1}{8}$ tsp. cayenne pepper
   $\frac{3}{4}$ cup flour or bread crumbs
   $\frac{1}{2}$ cup oil

Beat first nine ingredients together to make batter. Dip liver slices in batter, then in flour or crumbs. Pan fry in oil until brown.

My boys weren't fooled. They fed it to the dog, and when she died, they resorted to stuffing it in the waistband of their underwear to get away from the table.

BOOKS

Thundering Sneakers. Garden City, N.Y.: Doubleday, 1981.

Retreads. Garden City, N.Y.: Doubleday, 1985.

Just As We Were: A Narrow Slice of Texas Womanhood. Austin: University of Texas Press, 1996.

Paula Mitchell Marks

*Paula Mitchell Marks focuses on Western
and Southwestern themes in her nonfiction
books. She has received awards for each
of her three histories.*

Paula Mitchell Marks

I once heard a talk by Paula Mitchell Marks about how the Myers-Briggs Personality Profiles apply to the writing process. For those of you who share my profound ignorance of psychological dogma (not to mention my skepticism, which I admit is probably the result of ignorance), I'll give it to you in a pecan shell. (I thought it might offend someone if I used the word "nut" in that last sentence.) Anyway, according to the Myers-Briggs schema, we all prefer certain ways of conducting our lives. These habits, if you will, can be divided into four categories: (1) how we derive our energy—extrovert versus introvert; (2) how we work with information—sensing versus intuiting; (3) how we make decisions—thinking versus feeling; and (4) how we approach tasks—judging versus perceiving.

As Dr. Marks explained the preferences as they relate to her creative writing students—she teaches adults who are returning to college—I was struck by a couple of things. First, she was able to find something positive about every single preferred pattern. She was able to see the negative side, too, of course, but she stressed the positive aspects of each pattern. Second, her approach to teaching seemed particularly peaceful. As she concluded her talk, the relationship between her tolerance for all personality types and her peacefulness dawned on me. As a writing teacher, she is not trying to change anyone or control anyone. She knows that the creative process is as individual as a fingerprint and that it must be nurtured and reinforced, not changed or controlled. Her peacefulness comes from the belief that there is no such thing as the right way or the wrong way. I only hope her students realize how fortunate they are to have her as a teacher.

Paula Mitchell Marks

CARRIE'S SUSTAINING CHICKEN SOUP

I find most soups as unappealing as swampwater, especially those with a host of ingredients pureed into nothingness. At the other end of the spectrum—and almost as bad—are those watery concoctions delivered to one's table at Mexican restaurants with a whole chicken breast or a big, thick corn cob plopped into the middle. In my opinion, a soup should be creamy (but not too), with recognizable but not pet-rock-size ingredients.

When my daughter Carrie was small, we had a Winnie-the-Pooh picture book that showed Pooh's friend Rabbit making a Sustaining Soup. Carrie and I pored again and again over the picture of the cozy tree-trunk kitchen with its pleasant disarray. Rabbit, whose scrawny body looked as if it certainly could use something sustaining, presided over a steaming pot, adding lovely bright carrots and milk-white potatoes.

Carrie and I set out to make a Sustaining Soup of merit, adapting a chicken soup recipe from the First United Methodist Church of Austin's cookbook. We approached the project with some creative abandon, so it's hard to specify amounts. But the following—especially with some good homemade bread on the side—should satisfy a hungry group of six or seven.

Ingredients:
8 chicken breasts, cut in strips
2 cans chicken noodle soup (Carrie's favorite)
5 or 6 potatoes, cut in chunks (yes, I know it's odd to have
    noodles and potatoes together, but that's the way we make it)
8 carrots, cut in chunks
2 tbs. salt
Parsley (as much as you like)
Basil (as much as you like)
Half a stick of margarine
About $\frac{2}{3}$ cup flour
About 2 cups milk (I use skim, and it works fine)

First, fry the chicken strips in a little oil in a deep pot. Then add the chicken noodle soup and 4 soup-cans of water. Add potatoes and carrots, the salt, parsley, and basil. Bring to a boil and simmer on low for 45 minutes. Add the margarine, flour, and milk and continue to heat just until the broth thickens.

This is a soup to warm you through a Texas norther, but it also satisfies as the sun sets on an August scorcher.

BOOKS

Turn Your Eyes Toward Texas. College Station: Texas A&M University Press, 1989.

And Die in the West. New York: Morrow, 1989.

Precious Dust. New York: Morrow, 1994.

Hands to the Spindle. College Station: Texas A&M University Press, 1996.

Surviving on the Texas Frontier. Austin, Tex.: Eakin Press, 1996.

Sunny Nash

Sunny Nash is an essayist and short-story
writer. Her first full-length book
was published in 1996.

Sunny Nash

⤳

Sunny Nash now lives in California, but she grew up in a poor, emphatically segregated neighborhood in Bryan, Texas. In her book, she describes her childhood through a series of deceptively bland incidents which, when taken alone, seem as inconsequential as the flick of a wrist, but when considered together provide a sharp-lined drawing of what it was like to grow up before the civil rights movement. And she tells her story without a shred of vindictiveness or smugness.

My favorite passage is from a chapter entitled "Two, Four, Six, Eight!" The title comes from the first line of a taunt directed at African-American children by their classmates during the initial stages of integration in Bryan. Ms. Nash writes:

"Jumpy black-and-white pictures on the television assured me that I'd be arrested if I tried to eat in a restaurant downtown. I didn't care about eating at a restaurant. I just wanted to be able to use the restroom when my mother and I were out shopping. Because I loved my teachers at Washington Elementary, I wasn't interested in going to any other schools. I just wanted to be issued a textbook that had all the pages."

All the pages. So many of us in the white middle class took that, and so much more, for granted.

Sunny Nash
BIGMAMA'S MYSTERIOUS
ROSE WATER SPLASH

My grandmother's skin always had the delicate and intoxicating aroma of fresh-cut roses, and the finely polished texture of her seventy-year-old complexion was not too different from the skin of my own ten-year-old face.

In fact, my family has the kind of skin many people envy and some even worship. Born in 1949, I've been asked about everything from plastic surgery to what kind of deal I'd struck with the Devil to keep my face from aging.

My grandmother told me, "No matter how awkwardly your features are arranged on your face or what color the skin on your face may be, if the skin on your face is flawless, then your face is divine."

Is it in the genes?

Not!

Even as a child, I knew that my grandmother, whom everyone called Bigmama, must have been in the kitchen cooking up some skin magic with those roses. She grew lots of roses in different colors but did not tend them for their appearance, like the dainty porcelain ladies perched in the pages of magazine gardens.

Bigmama's gangly rose bushes grew under our windows that faced the street. Although our segregated Candy Hill neighborhood in northeast Bryan, Texas, was not plagued with crime in the 1950s, my grandmother was a most cautious woman who reminded herself, "If burglars try to come in, they will not have an easy time making it through these windows."

Hah!

Protection was the last thing on Bigmama's mind when she plucked her roses from their thick thorny stems.

About once a month in the spring and summer, our kitchen and the kitchens of our neighbors became laboratories for rose water splashes, sudsy complexion bars, and herbal treatments for problem skin, nails, and scalps. Bigmama's rose water splash, however, was not the complicated concoction of expensive chemicals one might imagine. In those days, everything except food and the most basic of clothing were a luxury to us.

Petals of one medium to large rose
Two cups tap water
One-quarter cup clear rubbing alcohol

In a small sauce pan, bring water to a boil.
Drop rose petals into boiling water.
Reduce heat, cover and simmer for ten minutes.
Remove from heat.
Allow to cool before stirring in the alcohol.
Store in a cool place in glass bottles with lids, stoppers, or corks.

This recipe can be doubled, tripled, or quadrupled, depending on how much rose water you wish to prepare in advance or give away as gifts. Try different colors of roses. Although the properties that enhance skin are the same, each color has a distinct fragrance. Place a rosebud or fresh petals in the bottle to indicate which color of flower the rose water was extracted from. Use rose water as a cleanser on a cotton ball or as a refreshing astringent after washing the face, after deep cleansing with facial mask, or after a light scrub.

When I was growing up, no one I knew could afford to buy cosmetics. They made their own beauty products from things in the kitchen mixed with things they picked from their yard because certainly no one could stretch a modest budget to buy chemicals. Who even knew where to buy chemicals anyway? The women who lived along the narrow dirt roads of my neighborhood did their laundry in the backyard by hand in a tub with a rub-board and homemade soap. These same women, though, had a soft sultry beauty that was matched only by the grace with which they went about their unfortunate lives.

BOOKS

Bigmama Didn't Shop at Woolworth's. College Station: Texas A&M
   University Press, 1996.

Naomi Shilab Nye

Naomi Shihab Nye is a highly acclaimed poet
and world traveler. She is known for her
insight and skillful use of metaphor.

Naomi Shihab Nye

There are many differences between good politicians and good teachers, of course, but the one I find most glaring is the way the two different camps handle questions. When asked a question—say, about how he suggests solving a problem—the good politician launches into an impassioned, exquisitely phrased response which may or may not answer the question but which most surely inspires his listeners, at least for the moment. The politician's words are offered in exchange for a vote or a contribution.

In contrast, the good teacher, like Naomi Nye, begins by making sure that she fully understands the question, asking a few questions of her own if need be. She then launches into an impassioned, exquisitely phrased response that, in addition to inspiring her pupils, truly does answer the question. Furthermore, that spark of inspiration doesn't float away with the balloons or fizzle with the fireworks, but grows. Like all good teachers, Naomi Nye expects nothing in return for her suggestion. It is an unqualified gift.

Ms. Nye is the quintessential teacher. She listens intently to her pupils' questions, sometimes straining forward, not to hear better but to grasp better the nuance of the problem. Then, in her contralto speaking voice, accentuated by hand motions as graceful and precise as those of a dancer, she goes to work. If you are enjoying a day-long class with Ms. Nye, she is as energetic in the late afternoon as she was at nine that morning. The only indication that the day is, indeed, winding down is that a few sprigs of hair have escaped her thick, dark braid. And her energy is infectious. You want to draw close and listen, because you begin to share her conviction that writing—a process she describes as gathering a few threads together so that they make some sense—is at least as important to a person's well-being as food and shelter. At least.

Naomi Shihab Nye's

HUMMUS

First of all, I take no credit for this recipe. I'm just a conveyor belt from one culture to another. My Austin friend, Arabic chef *extraordinaire* and writer Jim Shahin, describes his mixed Lebanese/Texana cookery as Tex-Leb or Leb-Tex, so consider this simplified version of the Palestinian staple food my Pal-Tex or Tex-Pal offering, adapted from my immigrant dad Aziz Shihab's methods. Many of his other recipes are included in his book, *A Taste of Palestine* (San Antonio: Corona Press, 1993).

Hey, pals! I don't want you to buy an inflated-price, already-prepared little tub of this delicious item in your refrigerated grocery bin ever again! Do that only if you're desperate. When you see how cheap and easy *hummus* is to make, you'll wonder, as I do, how anyone can mark the price up so high.

The following recipe will make enough *hummus* for an appetizer to serve four people. It is easy to double the amount of the recipe, or triple it. A very ravenous individual, however, could polish this whole thing off as a main course. Vegetarians appreciate it, since it is high-protein. It makes a wonderful late breakfast, lunch, or dinner. My grandmother ate it all her life and lived to be 106.

Hummus also is great to take to balmy Texas potluck gatherings, since it looks attractive spread out on a plate, everyone seems to like it, and it won't suffer from not being refrigerated.

What You Need:

1 can garbanzos (also known as chickpeas) — drain can, but save juice in a separate bowl in case you need it

2 garlic cloves (medium size, or one, if it is one of those plump ones)

3 tbs. tahini (sesame paste, available at imported food stores and some larger grocery stores — you may keep this in your pantry after opening, it does not have to be refrigerated)

1 tbs. or more olive oil

juice of 1 medium lemon

salt to taste

My feeling is—you pitch all these things into a blender and turn it on, first low, then high. You have to turn the blender on and off a few times and use a spatula to distribute the thickness and blend evenly. If too thick, add a small amount of the juice from the chickpea can or a little more lemon or olive oil. (You will find yourself throwing most of the juice away or saving it for soup later.)

My father's more traditional method is to heat up the garbanzo beans in their own liquid in a saucepan, simmering them for about 10–15 minutes, which is supposed to make them more pliable. Then he drains them, puts them into a big bowl and smashes them with a potato masher, adding all the other ingredients, along with a little of the liquid for texture. *Hummus* made this way is chunkier than *hummus* made in a blender. Do it the way you like it.

(My mother once had a friend who believed in removing the skin from each garbanzo bean before making *hummus,* to fight against possible flatulence caused by eating beans and peas. I think this is way, way over the line.)

Right before serving, you spread the *hummus* out on a large flat plate and drizzle it with olive oil, leaving a small, round pool in the center. Some people just serve it plain in a cereal bowl, but flattened is much more attractive. Sprinkle paprika on for color and add Mediterranean marinated olives, chopped parsley, half-moon slivers of raw onion, grilled onions, toasted pine nuts, or pickles for decoration. (Personally I think you can decorate with whatever you like, but recently I tried to add sliced cucumbers, and my father said, "No! No! No!")

Serve with warmed triangles of pita bread or corn chips (this is the Tex part).

As they say in the Middle East—*Sahtein!* Good appetite! Enjoy!

And buy a thicker notebook for your memoirs. You'll be 106 before you know it.

BOOKS

This Same Sky. New York: Four Winds Press, Macmillan, 1992.

Red Suitcase. Brockport, N.Y.: BOA Editions, 1994.

Sitti's Secrets. New York: Simon & Schuster, 1994.

Benito's Dream Bottle. New York: Simon & Schuster, 1995.

The Tree Is Older Than You Are. New York: Simon & Schuster, 1995.

Words Under the Words. Portland, Oreg.: Far Corner Books, 1995.

I Feel a Little Jumpy Around You. New York: Simon & Schuster, 1996.

Never in a Hurry. Columbia: University of South Carolina Press, 1996.

Habibi. New York: Simon & Schuster, 1997.

Lullaby Raft. New York: Simon & Schuster, 1997.

Laurence Parent

Laurence Parent is well known to most Texans
for his outdoor photography. He has also
written numerous books specializing in
landscape, travel, and nature subjects.

Laurence Parent

Regardless of how well Laurence Parent writes, it is his unmatched outdoor photography for which he is lionized. This is as it should be, for two reasons. First, as we all know, a picture is worth a thousand words. Laurence has published a jillion photographs, which—correct me if my math's wrong—is the equivalent of a thousand jillion words. He's going to have to get cracking on the computer if he plans to best that number. Second, it's no fair that he has two talents. No fair! *No fair!* I think we should make a rule that you can't be good at two things, and, if you are, then you have to choose one that your name is linked to.

Although I later met Laurence Parent at cluster book signings (where a group of authors simultaneously sign their books for eager book buyers or, failing that, commiserate about the time wasted by book signings), during the four years that I was gallivanting around the Hill Country doing research for my travel book, I never crossed paths with him. However, I talked to a number of people—mainly Texas Parks and Wildlife Department staff—who had met him. Since Laurence Parent is a celebrated name among nature and outdoor enthusiasts, everyone was eager to tell me about him. Over and over, they described how this skinny fellow, kinda quiet but real friendly, would haul this ungodly heavy equipment all over the place and then spend half the day checking first this and then that before he got down to taking snapshots. Every last person that I talked to admired his scrupulosity and assiduity, even if those were not the words they used. Those are also not words Laurence would ever use, because his writing is as precise and unencumbered as his photographs. Focused. That's the word I'm looking for. His writing is focused.

Laurence Parent's

EAST TEXAS STEW

If Deborah Douglas had known about my culinary qualifications, she might not have asked me to contribute to a cookbook. It's not that I'm a total loss in the kitchen—I can follow a recipe—it's just that cooking falls pretty low on my list when it comes to recreational activities. Without spending much time in the kitchen, it's hard to be creative. So I considered doing an essay on the fine points of peeling the corner back on a microwave dinner or the art of pouring milk on cold cereal, but figured that wouldn't wash. Next I considered camp cooking—I do a lot of camping for my writing and photography work—but opening a can of Dinty Moore stew and dumping it in a pot on the Coleman stove wasn't going to fly either.

In desperation, with the cookbook's deadline approaching, I enlisted my wife Patricia. Like me, she tends to be very busy and not inclined to spend hours puttering around a stove. However, she is a little more creative than yours truly. First I "borrowed" a recipe from my mother-in-law, Patsie Caperton, and then my wife tinkered with it in the kitchen. The result we called East Texas Stew because my mother-in-law grew up in East Texas. No surprise, it's a vast improvement over Dinty Moore.

Don't hesitate to alter the recipe to taste (or to use up whatever leftovers are in the refrigerator). Personally, if this were my recipe, I'd dump the turnip, but my wife swears that it gives flavor to the stew. So we left it in. We've made this stew several times, and no two batches have been quite the same. Probably the key ingredient is the V-8 juice used as part of the stock. So don't change that ingredient, even if you change everything else.

Ingredients:

1 46-ounce can V-8 juice
2 cups chicken broth
2 cups beef broth
1 lb. stew meat or venison
1 egg
½ cup milk

1 cup flour
vegetable oil
4 medium-sized potatoes
1 large yellow onion
1 small turnip
8 ounces carrots, chopped
½ celery bunch, chopped
8 ounces mushrooms, sliced
1 hot pepper
1 tsp. garlic powder
½ tsp. Tabasco sauce
½ tsp. vinegar
½ tsp. cumin
½ tsp. thyme
½ tsp. chili powder
1 tbs. black pepper

Heat the beef and chicken broth in a large (eight-quart or similar) pot. Slice the carrots, celery, potatoes, onion, turnip, and mushrooms. Add a little vegetable oil to a frying pan, and sauté the sliced mushrooms in it. When done, add the mushrooms, the other sliced vegetables, and the V-8 juice to the broth in the pot. Add garlic powder, Tabasco sauce, cumin, vinegar, thyme, chili powder, and black pepper. Throw in the jalapeño or similar pepper. Unless you have taste buds of iron, don't forget to fish the pepper back out of the stew after it's done cooking. Otherwise, sooner or later, you'll have a mouthful of fire.

In a small bowl, mix egg and milk together. Dip the stew meat or venison pieces in the liquid. Put flour on a plate, and coat the meat with it. Add more vegetable oil to the frying pan and heat. Place the meat in the pan and fry until the batter is brown. Remove the meat and pat the grease off with a paper towel. Put the meat in the pot, cover, and cook for two to three hours at low to medium heat. If you like your stew spicier, use additional spices or substitute spicy V-8.

This stew is good right out of the pot, but it also freezes well. This recipe makes a large amount, so you may want to freeze some. For camping trips, put the stew in a plastic container and freeze. When you leave, put the frozen container in an ice chest, where it can help keep other items cool. When you're ready, thaw it out and cook over your campfire or stove. It tastes even better outdoors—especially when compared to my usual camping chow.

BOOKS

Capulin Volcano National Monument. Tucson, Ariz.: Southwest Parks and Monuments Association, 1991.

Hiking New Mexico. Helena, Mont.: Falcon Press, 1991.

Flavor of the Hill Country. Tucson, Ariz.: Southwest Parks and Monuments Association, 1992.

Gila Cliff Dwellings National Monument. Tucson, Ariz.: Southwest Parks and Monuments Association, 1992.

Hiking Texas. Helena, Mont.: Falcon Press, 1992.

Big Bend of the Rio Grande. Big Bend Park, Tex.: Big Bend Natural History Association, 1993.

Big Thicket National Preserve. Tucson, Ariz.: Southwest Parks and Monuments Association, 1993.

Chickasaw National Recreation Area. Tucson, Ariz.: Southwest Parks and Monuments Association, 1993.

Lake Meredith National Recreation Area. Tucson, Ariz.: Southwest Parks and Monuments Association, 1993.

Chiricahua National Monument. Tucson, Ariz.: Southwest Parks and Monuments Association, 1994.

Scenic Driving New Mexico. Helena, Mont.: Falcon Press, 1994.

Austin. Houston: Gulf Publishing, 1995.

The Hill Country. Houston: Gulf Publishing, 1995.

Scenic Driving Texas. Helena, Mont.: Falcon Press, 1995.

Texas. Portland, Oreg.: Graphic Arts Center Publishing, 1995.

Hiking Big Bend National Park. Helena, Mont.: Falcon Press, 1996.

Santa Fe. Houston: Gulf Publishing, 1996.

Official Guide to Texas State Parks. Austin: University of Texas Press/Texas Parks and Wildlife Press, 1997.

Scenic Driving Wyoming. Helena, Mont.: Falcon Press, 1997.

Billy Porterfield has worked widely in the field of journalism. While writing for newspapers, magazines, television, and radio, he has acquired numerous honors and awards.

Billy Porterfield

I once attended an Austin Writers' League nonfiction workshop given by Billy Porterfield. So that he could better gear his remarks, he asked us to tell our name, what we'd written or wanted to write, and to let him know if there was some particular aspect of nonfiction writing that we wanted to talk about. A beautiful, sad-eyed, articulate woman confided that her desire (and need) to write might be a sequela of her recent nervous breakdown. After she spoke for a few minutes—Mr. Porterfield never interrupted her—he alluded to a similar rough spot that he had been through. With his characteristic sly, unflinching sense of humor, he told us about how he had come to know that he was jiggling aloose. He then turned to the beautiful lady and said gently, "You're gonna be okay. You'll be fine."

I don't know how much time and money the beautiful lady had spent on therapy. I can't say how much I've spent in the past and will most likely spend in the future on therapy, but I do know that Billy Porterfield's candor and dues-paid kindness had to be worth a lot to the beautiful lady, because they were worth a lot to me.

With few exceptions, writers accept from the start that we're not going to get rich writing. Most of us have day jobs to make the truck payments and scrunch in writing between our other obligations. I once heard a writer say that if she won the Texas lottery, she wouldn't buy a mansion or a full-size Cadillac. Instead, she would simply continue writing until she had spent it all. If not for a stack of gold, what then do writers hope for? I think it's fair to say that most aspire to be like Billy Porterfield and to have the skill and heart to say what people need to hear.

Billy Porterfield

A SMALL-TIME CANNIBAL'S RECIPE
FOR VEGETARIAN RUE

That Dallas fall, I watched her and Chantal Westerman gorge themselves on fettuccini at Gitana's on McKinney Avenue. The next noon
she was across the street at Ciro's, stuffing on Sicilian sandwich pizza—
her divine recipe. That night she was at The Grape on Greenville,
washing down *tournedos Bernaise* with a fine French Bordeaux.

Odd. You couldn't call her fat. She was indeed a large woman with
a monumental figure, too much for Vogue certainly, even Playboy,
but just right for Rubens and Renoir. I could see those two great
voluptuaries reading across the centuries that separated them, grap-
pling with one another over which would paint her naked. Renoir
would have won. Charlotte was too placid and pretty for Rubens. It's
true that the bones in her face were a little proud for Renoir, but he
would have brushed over that and buried himself in her pink flesh.

"Pierre," an admirer once asked him, "how do you know when you
have finished one of your nudes?"

"When I want to pinch her," he replied.

Or, better, feast upon her, I thought. You see, I couldn't get Charlotte Parker out of my mind. She was, it seemed to me from across all
those dining rooms, a divine endomorph, a goddess to the slower
rhythms of earth and Epicurean delight. But how much of this was
my fancy? It was hard to say. She was inscrutable, a great, strawberry
blonde enigma.

But I was undaunted. The writer in me wanted to approach and
draw her out, to capture the mysterious character that lay sentient in
all that rich array of womanly protoplasm. Surely she was not of our
anemic gnawing time, when every Adam wants his Eve spare as a rib.
God and her genes had conspired to make of her a big, handsome
woman, and she had taken that inheritance and had nurtured it well
without a downward look at the scales. The only beauties in our society who dared to be so full and abundant were opera divas and the
women in Federico Fellini's cinematic dreams. Brava, Charlotte, brava.

The more I learned about her, the more I wanted to know.

It was fitting that she turned out to be a part-owner of the very restaurants she frequented. Eventually she and her partner, Kathy McDaniels, closed Gitana's and Ciro's so they could give all their attention to The Grape. This narrowed Charlotte's daily rounds, making her an easier target for my professional intentions. It is amazing the lengths a writer will go for material. I moved into a flat over The Grape to get the goods on my new landlady.

I learned she had a bench press and that she didn't put potted plants on it. She actually lifted weights (bench press 120 pounds).

I learned she was 5 feet 8 and weighed 162 pounds, and that she had been that size as early as the sixth grade. Her IQ almost matched her weight, which meant that as a schoolgirl Charlotte had been a social outcast. She was left to eating moon pies and reading J. D. Salinger and Walker Percy. I made a note to myself: Match literary wits with her, then talk about food.

I learned that at ten she had been a religious fanatic, but that by twelve she was espousing atheism. Best leave that alone. Whoa. Maybe not. She was said to see in cannibalism the same transubstantiations Christians seek in the feasts of the Sacred Heart and the Eucharist.

At last, I finagled an invitation to dine one weekend evening at her home on the gentrified Eastside. I fasted for two days in anticipation of a great culinary experience. In my daydreams lamb was on my mind. Maybe she would open with asparagus in a vinaigrette sauce. Then we would move to the main course, poached leg of lamb with dill and capers, mashed potatoes and green salad. A St. Emilion wine, perhaps. And Southern pecan pie. We would retire to the living room, sniff brandy, and talk of the rise and fall of theme restaurants and the decline of the West.

It was after a word-to-the-wise from her chef at The Grape, Michael Blackwell, that Cornish game hens began to simmer in what I can't call nightmares since I enjoyed them so much. Blackwell had said Charlotte's game hen fricassee with a French New Guinea twist was to be savored. Her recipe that he gave me underwent a strange alchemy in my night sweats. I became the chef with tom-tom and bone in my nose, and all 162 pounds of Charlotte the plump game chick plucked from safari. I never will forget the ingredients that went into that pagan ecstasy.

In a No. 3 tin tub or iron pot greased with coconut butter and fired by sandalwood coals and libidinal dreams, add the following ingredients:

Brimming ardors of expectation
12.5 magnums of dry table wine
12.5 magnums of Mamberamo river water
Small basket of spiced cobra

After broth is boiling, let coals relax the pot to a simmer. Then add one plump (160 pounder ideal) game chick, loosely stuffed and trussed with wild rice, grapes; her body rubbed with coconut butter and dredged in sagu palm flour.

Simmer ingredients until game chick is tender.

Add cuts of sugar cane stalks to taste.

Serve a whole tribe with rice, nuts, and fresh grapes.

After four sweaty nights of this ritual, I was ashamed to appear at her door. But, of course, on the appointed night right on the hour, I was there.

As soon as Charlotte admitted me, I noticed there was something different about her. But I couldn't put my finger on it. "You've changed," I said.

"Can you believe it?" she said. "I've lost 15 pounds in the last 17 days."

My God! Was I the culprit? Had she been privy to my shameless dreams? My mouth fell open.

"I'm fasting," she said brightly.

My heart started up in relief, then sank.

"That's wonderful," I said lamely, kissing off the leg of lamb and most certainly the plump game chick.

"Yes," she went on. "I haven't had a bite to eat since June 4. That night I ate so much I swore off food. Michael Blackwell and I ate at Sh-Boom, the health food place on Lovers Lane. He treated me to such a feast that I had to walk around the park before I could breathe freely. Never again, I said, and I've lived on bottled water and juices."

"Aren't you overdoing it a bit? That sounds depleting and dangerous."

"I've never felt better in my life. I've never had so much energy. Of course I can't keep fasting. I'll start eating fruits and vegetables in a few days. But I'll keep it a mystic's fare. My goal is to lose 35 pounds by my 35th birthday, which is August 27. So I've got 20 pounds to go. I'll make it."

"But why?" I protested.

"Because I was tired of being an overweight, lazy slob," she said. "I want to get back to my UT beauty queen weight."

I felt betrayed.

"I thought you weighed 162 pounds when you were in the sixth grade," I said.

"I did, and I hated it. But when I reached high school I slimmed down and became a yearbook beauty and all that."

"I thought you were a social outcast," I said.

"I was, but not later at Lamar High and the University of Texas. I married a star fullback and did the whole country club thing. The marriage didn't work. It was just surface. After that I buried myself in work and food."

"You didn't eat for the joy of it?"

"It was a substitute for not participating in life. I'm a committed vegetarian now. The thought of eating meat sickens me. We weren't meant to be carnivorous. We've flat teeth for grinding grass, like horses and cows, not pointed teeth for tearing flesh like dogs. Besides, our intestines are too long for digesting meat. It putrefies by the time we're ready to eliminate it."

For some reason, that last bit embarrassed me.

It was a terribly hot night. I began to feel queasy. I thought of Robinson Jeffer's poem about the deepest meaning of original sin. He believed its origins went back to the time animals first began eating one another.

"You look like you could stand some refreshment," Charlotte said. "I'm having sparkling water over ice for dinner tonight. Will you join me?"

"Might as well," I said, with a grand irony she would never know until now. "I've been feasting till morning most sinfully the last few nights."

BOOKS

LBJ Country. Garden City, N.Y.: Doubleday, 1965.

The Book of Dallas. Garden City, N.Y.: Doubleday, 1977.

A Loose Herd of Texans. College Station: Texas A&M University Press, 1978.

Texas Rhapsody: Memories of a Native Son. New York: Holt, Rinehart and Winston, 1981.

The Greatest Honky-Tonks in Texas. Dallas: Taylor Publishing, 1983.

Fathers and Daughters. Dallas: Taylor Publishing, 1988.

Diddy Waw Diddy: Passage of an American Son. New York: HarperCollins, 1994.

*Cactus Pryor began his career as a
broadcaster at the end of World War II
and has been a popular humorist on radio
and a mainstay on the national lecture
ever since. His books are compilations
of his best radio essays.*

Cactus Pryor

The most challenging part of preparing this book was convincing the authors that they wanted to contribute a recipe. I made participation as simple as possible by compiling an author packet with the following items: cover letter, sample chapter, stamped bounce-back card to let me know whether or not they wanted to participate, return-addressed priority-mail envelope, copyright release forms, author information sheet, index cards for signatures, and a checklist to consult when they were returning all the items. I sent the packet by priority mail. Silly, naive me envisioned it this way. The author would receive the packet, immediately (and eagerly, maybe even breathlessly) return the bounce-back card, followed in a few weeks by his or her recipe, a photo, signature cards, author information sheet, and release forms. Simple. Or so thought silly, naive me.

My communications with Cactus Pryor, if not exactly typical of those with most of the participating authors, at least demonstrate the challenges involved when you're working with a busy celebrity who recently published a book. I wrote Mr. Pryor three letters—funny, chatty, nice letters—before he sent me his recipe. Period. No release forms, etc. (To this humorous, sharp-witted, and indomitable man's credit, he finally did answer me, which is more than I can say for some of the authors I invited—yes, invited, not asked, but *invited*—to participate. I consider it ill breeding, plain and simple, when someone doesn't see fit to answer an invitation.)

But back to Mr. Pryor. I then sent him a fourth letter and a second packet of release forms, etc., and a second return-addressed priority-mail envelope. I sent this packet by priority mail. He promptly returned all the necessary items in the envelope I had provided. You're wondering why I didn't pester him for an interview so that I could write something about him like I'm doing for the other authors? Well, for one thing, I don't think I could have afforded the postage. More important, though, I had used up all my funny, chatty, and nice remarks in my first four letters.

Cactus Pryor's
MEXICAN LASAGNA

All right, Deborah . . . nag, nag, nag. I always give in. Trouble is, I am to cooking what Packwood is to chastity. I ain't very experienced. I do open a mean can and can open a ziploc with the best of them. Give me a box of Pioneer Flour Biscuit and Pancake mix and I can turn out a breakfast that's better than most people deserve. Otherwise, my cooking skills are all devoted to one dish which I call Mexican Lasagna. Here's how it happens:

Two pounds of ground sirloin. Buy it.

Toasted tortillas. Buy 'em . . . slap a dab of butter and salt on 'em, then toast them till they're Tex-Mex crispy.

Lowfat cottage cheese, small curd. Buy it.

Sharp cheddar cheese. Buy it already shredded unless you get your kicks shredding cheese.

You've already got chili powder in your house. If you don't, you won't be interested in this dish anyway.

Onions. Buy 'em and chop 'em.

Pecans. Shell 'em if they're not already. We want halves here.

Pimientos. Get some. I think they're all red.

Okay, here we go. Cook the meat 'til done in a frying pan. Salt and pepper it as you go and add a liberal . . . excuse me, more than conservative amount of chili powder. I'm allergic to garlic, but if you're not, why not? When meat is near done, add enough tomato sauce to give it the consistency of a good Italian meat sauce. Add onions. Let it cook awhile 'til all the stuff is compatible.

Second verse: Line one of those rectangular thick clear cooking dishes that won't burst in an oven with a layer of the crispy tortillas. Cover them with a layer of what you made in the frying pan. Then cover that with a thin layer of cottage cheese and then sprinkle a serious amount of cheddar cheese on top of that.

Dab a bunch of green olive halves on all of that. Black olives are okay, too. If you're feeling feisty, add some jalapeños. Push some pecans down here and there. When you've done that, cover all that you can see with more tortillas.

Then just repeat all above until you've done three different layers. On the last one, add a little more cottage cheese than you've added below, and stick some of those green olive halves and lots of red pimentos and pecans around, 'cause this is the top of the deal. The colors create a festive, Christmasy look.

Here's the best part of the deal. You want to fix all this before the party. Then stick it in the freezer. When the party's getting too wild, put it in the oven and heat it at a temperature that suits you. It was be ready to serve before you can say, "I need a doctor."

I take no responsibility for that which follows.

BOOKS

Inside Texas. Austin, Tex.: Shoal Creek Publishers, 1982.
Playback. Austin: University of Texas Press, 1995.

Clay Reynolds is a novelist and literary scholar. He has published numerous articles, essays, and reviews, most of which concern southwestern and Texan authors.

Clay Reynolds

Grousing with Clay Reynolds about the sheer awfulness of most book *sittings*—as I early on took to calling book signings—he told me the story of his most successful signing. At the request of his publisher, he appeared at a Dallas signing with a young man whose new novel had just been published. It turned out that Clay's tablemate was a local celebrity of sorts, having played football at Highland Park High School and later been a rather celebrated student at Southern Methodist University. Many well-dressed friends arrived to buy his book and formed a line that extended to the end of the aisle and out into the street. Being the polite yuppies that most of them were, they also cheerfully bought a copy of Clay's book as well, even though none of them had a clue who he was or what his book was about.

Things were going splendidly for the first twenty minutes—Clay estimates he sold several dozen books—until a vague acquaintance shuffled up. She proceeded to stand there for an hour, droning on about her plans to write a book. Besides blocking his view of the heretofore magnanimous book buyers in front of his co-signer, Clay says, "She was also remarkably obnoxious in manner, and, not to put too fine a point on it, she looked like a bag lady." The line of Dallas yuppies arced away, and Clay never sold another book.

Still, though, windy bag lady notwithstanding, that evening broke his previous record of selling twelve books—and that had been after a reading. He ended his bittersweet success story with the somber estimation that he doesn't sell a single book at 65 percent of his signings. Somehow, in an admittedly pathetic sort of way, Clay's story cheers me up. Here he is, an award-winning novelist, doing no better at most book signings/sittings than I do.

Clay Reynolds's
TEX-MEX BREAKFAST

Most people who are real Texans by birth or at least by attitude know that a "Mexican breakfast" consists of a cup of black coffee and a cigarette. This isn't politically correct, but it's culturally accurate. Most of the things that are culturally accurate about Texas aren't politically correct. Never have been.

This is not, however, a recipe for a cup of black coffee and a cigarette, a breakfast that, by the way, is getting harder and harder to find in Texas's urban areas. In Austin and Arlington, it's extinct, in fact, insofar as café fare goes. You have to go to Fort Worth, or damn near it, to find a comfortable public place to sit down and read the morning paper anymore. The Health and Nutrition Police seem to have joined forces with the Politically Correct Police to squelch most everything about being a Texan or even just being in Texas that might give pleasure or elicit a smile. Pretty soon, we're going to have to go to Louisiana or Arkansas just to swear—or to find a beer that isn't served with a lime and doesn't require the drinker to wear a helmet.

Anyway, this is not a recipe for a cup of coffee and a cigarette. *Nor* is it a recipe for breakfast for the hard of arteries or the genteel of palate. It's also not for the Berkenstock and cable-knit sweater crowd who tend to think that whole-wheat tortilla chips, spinach enchiladas, and bean-sprout tacos are ethnic food. And it's not for those who think flour tortillas are preferable to corn. People who prefer flour tortillas and think "chicken *fajitas*" even makes sense belong to the same group that puts ketchup on hamburgers and beans in chili. These folks would be happier, I think, with a road map whereon the interstate highways out of the state have been highlighted for their more hasty progress back to whence they came—most likely, Colorado or California or New York City, where food is healthy and bland and unimaginative, and where "spicing" consists of opening a box of salt somewhere in the same county where they're cooking.

This is a Tex-Mex breakfast, meaning it can be cooked and served any time of the day or night, whenever appetite and a desire for something hearty and hot overcomes the desire to "eat right" or to avoid anything that's not low-calorie, low-fat, low-taste, and devoid of originality.

This is just plain good. And actually, it's pretty healthy, as stuff that's bad for you goes. And it feeds a bunch.

What's required is the following:

Four to six eggs at room temperature.
About two tablespoons of butter or, if you insist, margarine.
One Texas 1016 onion, chopped coarse. (Bermuda red will do.)
Two to three stalks of celery, chopped coarse.
About half a medium-sized bell pepper, chopped coarse.
One clove of garlic, chopped fine.
One quarter cup of black olives, sliced.
One quarter cup of green chilies, chopped fine.
Four large, fresh tomatoes, skinned and blanched; or one sixteen-ounce can of stewed tomatoes. Be sure they're well seined, but still moist.
A healthy dash of salt.
A healthy sprinkle of black pepper.
A dash of Worcestershire or however you spell it, but only a dash.
A half cup of finely shredded sharp cheddar cheese.
A nine- or twelve-inch cast-iron skillet.

The skillet is the most important item on the list. It must be *cast iron,* not aluminum, steel, glass, or any sort of non-stick, bright and shiny, fancy-dan, Yankeefied kitchen "chef's pan," not something coated with the same stuff they use on jet aircraft or the Space Shuttle or bullet-proof vests. This dish, like decent cornbread and well-fried bacon, requires old-fashioned, coal-black, and preferably rust-spotted cast-iron skillet, the kind you have to have a pot holder to handle when it's hot, the kind that weighs about as much as a Peterbilt transmission, the kind Grandma used to brain Grandpa with when he came stumbling in late with "liquor on his breath and lovin' on his mind," as the saying goes. The kind that's impossible to clean but which heats evenly and completely and which was designed to by-God cook with, not to hang on some artfully designed over-the-oven rack in some misguided attempt to get your kitchen featured in *Southern Living*. If one of these suckers falls off an overhead rack, you might wind up with a fractured skull; drop one, and you can break a toe. If you don't own one (shame on you!), they can be had cheap at most flea markets or old-fashioned hardware stores. No self-respecting Texas household is without at least three different sizes.

You can't fry catfish or chicken without one.

They're also handy for defense against cockroaches, rats, and the occasional mongrel dog, and they'll deflect a .357 Magnum slug at close range and still cook up a chicken fried steak and cream gravy that'd make a truck driver weep for joy. Try that with your fancy French copper-bottomed jobbie.

Anyway, get a cast-iron skillet to cook this dish.

Preheat the skillet and melt the butter or margarine, coating the bottom and the sides.

Sauté all chopped vegetables in the skillet in the butter or margarine until clear but still crisp. Add the tomatoes and the Worchestisshireer sauce, and stir occasionally until the vegetables are fully blended and the whole mess is steaming hot, actually bubbling a bit. Don't worry about any extra liquid forming from the tomatoes. You'll need it.

Use the spatula to form small "wells" in the bubbling vegetables at even "quarter-hour" intervals around the sides. Crack the eggs one at a time, careful not to break the yolks, trying to make sure that they are well away from the sides and are nestled into the small vegetable wells. Salt and pepper the yolks. I like to add a tiny drop of Padulo's Red or Green Sauce on each yolk, but Tabasco sauce will do.

Reduce heat to warm and cover. Cook for about four minutes or until the eggs are about three-quarters poached. If necessary, separate the vegetables gently to allow any uncooked portions of the egg whites to penetrate the entire concoction. Add the shredded cheese, sprinkling it generously over the whole thing, being sure to cover the eggs especially well. Re-cover and leave on warm until cheese is completely melted.

Remove to the table (a trivet is a good idea) and cut into quarters and serve directly from the skillet with a spatula. A steaming pile of fresh tamales goes well with it, as does a spicy salsa, which can be spooned over the top to taste; serve with heated corn tortillas, butter, and preserves of your choice. Sopapillas with honey are nice, if you want to go to the trouble. If tortillas are unavailable, use *another* cast-iron skillet and whip up a batch of Mexican cornbread. Serves four to six reasonably sober adults, two drunks, or one teenager.

For breakfast, fresh orange juice goes great with this; buttermilk is a wonderful complement; later in the day, beer washes it down well; in the evening, some people prefer margaritas. I find that black coffee and a cigarette are the best items for finishing it off; but if you must, go for your low-cal, high-fiber, protein-charged reconstituted fruit-drink, or Metamucil.

Tips:

Real cast-iron skillets almost never can be found with lids or covers. Here's a chance to put to good use one of those really expensive Belgian omelet pan lids somebody gave you and that you've been afraid to use for fear of ruining it. Just pop it on there. If it warps, it died in a good cause and can later be used as a water dish for the cat, an ashtray when you finally go back to smoking, or to replace a hubcap on a '64 Fairlane. But any skillet or pot lid will do. The cover needn't be tight, just enough to allow the eggs to poach, the cheese to melt.

Heartier appetites will require more eggs—say two per serving—and a twelve-inch skillet will accommodate up to eight hen fruit, but no more. It's usually best to try to cook them in pairs, rather than make six separate wells, though. If more food is needed, make a second skilletful at the same time. Too many eggs in too small a space prevents the mixture from cooking to a nice thick texture for serving. The idea is that it should come out almost like a slice of pie. Runny eggs (or broken yolks) ruin the dish, but don't overcook the yolks; hard eggs spoil it, too. I find that six eggs in a nine-inch skillet is pushing the combination to the limit.

You can't use too much cheese in this, but you can vary the type. Monterey Jack and Provolone make for interesting variations, as does Swiss or even Gouda. Soft cheeses don't work well, though. (We won't even *discuss* processed cheese or low-fat cheese or "cheese food.") The amounts of these alternatives may require some experimentation, as they don't all melt at the same rate or provide the same consistency when shredded.

Stronger tastes (cigar smokers, for example) may want more spice.

Using sliced jalapeños rather than the green chilies works well, or it might be desirable to substitute or add in addition some poblanos, red peppers, banana peppers, or other spices such as cilantro or basil for variety. Actually, you could just sauté a robust, homemade *pico de gallo,* then add the tomatoes. An Italian version can be achieved with Italian peppers and tomatoes, oregano, anchovies, and green olives. Pimentos also work nicely to add color and a slightly tart taste. And a German version could be accomplished by using sauerkraut and horseradish and well-sautéed, diced potatoes, rather than the other spices. Hashed browns make a good side dish, as do *frijoles* or *guacamole* salad.

For a party feed, say during the World Series, Superbowl, or next televised celebrity murder trial or presidential impeachment hearings, you could serve this with a side of homemade chili (no beans, for the love of Texas!), which could be ladled over the whole thing by each person according to taste and degree of appetite and propensity for dyspepsia. I've had as many as four skillets going at once, all coming out exactly together.

Cleaning up is a chore; just put the skillets out on the porch and let the dogs do the hard part, then pray for rain.

Never put a cast-iron skillet in a dishwasher.

The main thing is: play with it. I never make it exactly the same way twice, but it almost always comes out great and receives rave reviews, particularly late at night when folks are clamoring for a filling and nutritious if not entirely health-conscious meal. But it mostly works very well for "company breakfast," whether the company is Mexican, Yankee, Californian, Coloradan, or just plain Texan.

BOOKS

Agatite. New York: St. Martin's, 1986.
Stage Left: The Development of the American Social Drama. Troy, N.Y.: Whitston Press, 1986.
The Vigil. New York: St. Martin's, 1986.

Taking Stock: A Larry McMurtry Casebook. Dallas: Southern Methodist University Press, 1989.

Franklin's Crossing. New York: Dutton, 1992.

One Hundred Years of Heroes. Fort Worth: Texas Christian University Press, 1995.

Players. New York: Carroll & Graf, 1997.

Twenty Questions: A Writer's Guide. Dallas: Browder Springs Press, 1998.

Joyce Gibson Roach, who has published fiction, nonfiction, and musical drama, is a former president of the Texas Folklore Society and teaches courses in Southwestern and Western literature at Texas Christian University.

Joyce Gibson Roach

After two unpleasant exchanges with New Yorkers during a family vacation at Big Bend National Park, I decided that the river border we Texans need concern ourselves with is not the Rio Grande, but the Red River. (I'm sorry to be so ugly, but goda'mighty, New Yorkers can be rude.) Before I stand accused of being a provincial old patoot, let me make a suggestion. As part of their acculturation, recent immigrants to Texas must read the following five books: *A Natural State: Essays on Texas,* by Stephen Harrigan; *Texas My Texas,* by James Ward Lee; *In a Narrow Grave: Essays on Texas,* by Larry McMurtry; *The Edge of the West and Other Texas Stories,* by Bryan Woolley; and *This Place of Memory: A Texas Perspective,* a collection edited by Joyce Gibson Roach. And anyone who even so much as crosses the Red River for a visit (particularly New Yorkers heading toward Big Bend) must read the last book on the list, because this book, more than any other that I've run across, defines what it means to be a Texan. It does this by exploring the many levels and meanings of Texans' sense of place.

Joyce Roach is the first to admit that the term "sense of place" was reduced to a cliché in the late eighties and early nineties, as it became stylish to write about one's roots. The more rural the roots—and the more common the place—the better, or so it seemed. To sidestep this groove, she expanded "sense of place" beyond the reference to a physical location, to include being with another person or doing one's work or even embracing one's beliefs. To Joyce, "sense of place" means that which gives a person a sense of well-being: "We are all searching for that place of belonging, of safety, of peace; that locale where survival instincts and basic needs are fulfilled in a location that smells, yea verily, reeks of sanctuary because we hunger, figuratively and literally, for place."

After sharing this enlarged meaning with them, Joyce invited longtime writer friends to submit their work. And did they ever. The collection that resulted is magical. So magical, in fact, that it might even make rude New Yorkers stand still.

Nah.

Joyce Gibson Roach's
BIRTHDAY CAKE

(An excerpt from *Eats: A Folk History of Texas Foods*. Used by permission of Texas Christian University Press.)

Narrator: Three significant, portentous, historical events rife with worldwide implications marked my early life and are responsible for all that I am today—a peaceful, satisfied, calm, optimistic individual. The events were the Great Depression of the 1930s, World War II in the 1940s, and My Birthday Cake, which first appeared in 1936.

The Depression was a delightful affair and was superseded only by World War II in its calming and reassuring remembrances. I lived in Jacksboro, where we all had plenty of nothing in equal proportions, where we made our own entertainment and recreation, composed our own joy and sorrow, and voted in favor of joy whenever we could. Although I was an only child, I believed that the entire town was kin to me and hold that place responsible even today for the peculiar way I turned out. All occasions of war and peace were shared together. I was enveloped in such an insular wrapping of loving, caring, sharing, and giving for so many of my formative years that it was a terrible shock to find out much later in my life that the history books considered both the Depression and World War II horrible and devastating occurrences. Only My Birthday Cake remains untouched by either the history books or someone else's opinion.

As I said, I was an only child, but even that is not significant necessarily. The Depression and World War II were at that time the most effective birth control devices ever invented, and there were many only children in my town. Not any only child, however, anywhere in the town or in the world had a cake like mine because it was *mine*. The cake could not have been baked except in an extraordinary place. The place was a kitchen. There was bright yellow linoleum on the floor. Brighter yellow curtains were at the windows. Everything else was white, bright white. The cookbook stood out in black relief on the table, giving depth and perspective to white-on-yellow. Texture was added by rough woolen coats and mittens, wintertime textures thrown over the kitchen chairs. The room was, however, merely a setting, a stage, until the central presence entered the kitchen—Mother, Leading Lady.

It was the day before my birthday, December 17, 1944. (Curtain up; lights up on Mother and Joyce Ann at the kitchen table, center; other lights dim on set.)

Mother: Dust the pans, Joyce Ann. That's all you have to do. It's your job, birthday or not. Wash your hands first. Wash your hands! Read me the recipe. (Joyce Ann reads the recipe, but Mother is already pouring ingredients into a large mixing bowl, obviously familiar with the procedure.)

Joyce Ann:

Devil's Food Cake

1 egg
Pinch salt
1 cup sour milk
$1\frac{1}{4}$ cups sugar
$\frac{1}{2}$ cup shortening
4 tablespoons cocoa
1 teaspoon soda in milk (makes a cake darker in color and adds
   other good things to it)
$1\frac{1}{2}$ cups flour

Beat in the egg white separately.

Why do I always have to read the recipe? You already got it ready to put in the oven by the time I finish?

Mother: Because that way you learn something about cooking and practice reading out loud; someday you might want to talk in public or make a speech or something and then you would sorta know what do to. (Changing the subject.)

We're going to the show tonight. There are newsreels about the war. We have to go and look. We might see Fred. (She pours up the cake batter in the three pans; crosses to oven, kitchen-stage right.)

You didn't light the oven. Don't ever put a cake in a cold oven. The oven's got to be heated first, "350 degrees for thirty minutes," that's what the directions say. Now, we'll have to wait. (She strikes a match, holds it to the opening at the front of the open oven door, waits for the flame to catch and the "whoosh" that signals the catch, and returns to the table.)

Joyce Ann: (Taking bowls and spoons to the sink, also stage right, but not washing them.) We never have seen Uncle Fred yet, but we did see Mrs. Jones's boy, Willie, one time, didn't we? There was such a bunch of 'em and all in soldier suits. They all looked alike to me. I don't have any lessons tonight either. We won't do anything at school tomorrow but have our Christmas party. Did you bake the cookies for the party? Mary Jane's mother is supposed to bake a bunch, but you know we won't be able to eat 'em. I hope you made double. Couldn't we skip the movie part and just go in time for the newsreel? I've seen the movie three times. (Comes back to the table.)

Mother: No, we have to pay for the movie and not just the newsreel. We'll see all of it or else not get our money's worth. That would be wasteful not to see everything. The oven's hot. Carry one of those pans for me.

(Both go to oven, kitchen-stage right; Mother waits on Joyce Ann to put hers in first, then rearranges the pan to suit herself and puts in the other two pans, making comments such as "don't burn yourself," "put it more on the right side in the back," etc. Both return to table and Joyce Ann sits down.)

Joyce Ann: Tell me the story when Uncle Fred was home that Thanksgiving and we shot at the ducks and you said I could never go hunting again.

Mother: That's the silliest thing I ever heard of. I wasn't even along on that hunt. You were there. I just heard about it. You tell me, silly. (She closes the cookbook as she speaks and washes off the oilcloth with a wet dishrag.)

Joyce Ann: Yeah, but I was just a little kid and I don't remember how funny it was. Just Fred remembers how funny it was and he isn't here. Mother, is he ever coming home? Is he gonna get killed? I don't like my birthday or Christmas without him.

Mother: Of course, he's comin' home and he certainly isn't going to die. Wait a minute, let me check the cakes. (She goes to the oven, checks the cake, but continues to speak as she walks back to the table.) Let's see. It was Thanksgiving two years ago just before Fred went away to the Navy. You and him and your daddy went out to Audie Weir's place to hunt. You didn't get a thing, just tramped around all day in the woods picking up pecans. You must have had ten pounds of big ole Burketts for Mama Hartman and me to pick out. I never saw such a bunch of pecans, as if we needed any with a tree right in the backyard here. Well, anyway, the three of you put the guns in the back of the ole truck your daddy fixed up and called the "hoopee." (They both laugh.) Just about the time you got a bit past Audie's big tank, Fred hollered, "Stop, Dave! Stop the truck! There's ducks on the tank!" (Mother stops her story to get a pan with ingredients for the icing which have already been measured out and await cooking. She puts pan on the burner, after lighting it with a match; then turns off the oven, removes the cakes, and stands stirring the mixture.)

Joyce Ann: Tell the rest of it! That's not the funny part. Tell it all.

Mother: Well, he made ya'll get out, told you to be real quiet, and whispered that you all three had to crawl on your hands and knees across the icy ground up to the dam of the tank or else you'd scare the ducks. And you got the guns and . . .

Joyce Ann: (Joyce Ann giggles, puts her hand up to her mouth, and whispers) And—and then we did crawl over the dam and right down to the water and then Uncle Fred jumps up and shouts (Joyce Ann screams now), "Shoot, Dave, shoot!" And Daddy shot the gun, lost his balance, and fell full face into the tank and the ice cold water. And, and—he didn't hit one duck, not a one!

(Both Mother and Joyce Ann laugh until the tears come. Mother comes to the table with the icing and the cakes, and speaks, with tears still running down her cheeks.)

Mother: Read the directions for the icing, Joyce Ann. And then read me the baking directions and about how to grease the pans and how many it will serve. (She speaks quietly, barely above a whisper.)

Joyce Ann: But, Mother, the directions are always the same. You already cooked the icing.

Mother: Yes, Joyce, it is always the same. Some things always have to be the same, never different, never changed, or else how could we know how to cook or how to make it through—till Fred comes home?
  (Lights down on mother and daughter as Joyce Ann takes a tablespoon, scrapes the pan, and licks the spoon.)

Narrator:

Chocolate Icing

  2 cups sugar
  Pinch salt
  $\frac{3}{4}$ cup evaporated milk
  Lump of butter, the size of a walnut
  As much cocoa as desired

Cook to the soft ball stage. Then drop in butter and vanilla and wait until lukewarm to beat.

Baking Directions for the Cake

Bake at 350 degrees for 30 minutes. Cake is very light. Makes two layers unless you make three thin layers. Also a good cupcake recipe. Be sure to grease and flour the pans. If the icing gets too thick and tries to set up on you, add more evaporated milk. The icing could be made with cream, if you can afford it. The recipe doesn't call for it, but I would put in a teaspoon of vanilla in batter and icing too.
  This recipe was copied from Mother's black notebook-cookbook just the way she wrote it in 1936.
  Uncle Fred did come home. He took up his place as the storyteller once more. The scene of My Birthday Cake was repeated with a larger cast. My mother told me a secret about what made the cake batter taste so good, about something that was not in the recipe. She made me promise not to tell, but I'll tell you. Put a pinch, not a half-tea-

spoon even, of cinnamon in the cake batter. Just promise not to tell anyone else or she'll know I told the secret. She knows I never could keep my mouth shut about anything.

BOOKS

C. L. Sonnichsen. Boise, Idaho: Boise State University, 1979.

Texas and Christmas: A Collection of Traditions, Memories, and Folklore. Fort Worth: Texas Christian University Press, 1983.

Hoein' the Short Rows. Dallas: Southern Methodist University Press, 1987.

Eats: A Folk History of Texas Foods (with Ernestine Sewell Link). Fort Worth: Texas Christian University Press, 1989.

The Horned Toads' Christmas. Denton: Texanna Press, 1989.

The Cowgirls. Denton: University of North Texas Press, 1990.

Women of the West: An Anthology of Short Stories by Contemporary Western Women Writers. Garden City, N.Y.: Doubleday, 1990.

This Place of Memory: A Texas Perspective: A Collection. Denton: University of North Texas Press, 1992.

Ride for the Brand. Fort Worth: Texas Christian University Press, 1993.

New Trails: Twenty-three Original Stories of the West from Western Writers of America. Garden City, N.Y.: Doubleday, 1994.

Collective Heart: Texans in World War II. Austin, Tex.: Eakin Press, 1996.

Wild Rose: A Folk History of a Cross-Timbers Settlement. Virginia Beach, Va.: Donning Co., 1996.

Studies in the Western. Münster: German Association for the Study of the Western, 1997.

Elizabeth Silverthorne

Elizabeth Silverthorne is a free-lance writer
living in Salado. She has written stories for
children as well as articles and books for people
of all ages on various topics of Texas and
Southern history.

Elizabeth Silverthorne

My day job is being the pathologist at Southeast Baptist Hospital in San Antonio. This means that I am constantly looking for something under the microscope that I don't want to find. In a given week, it is not uncommon for me to diagnose between five and ten cases of cancer. When one of those patients is someone I know and care about—like a thirty-nine-year-old medical technician who works in my laboratory—I need a bedtime story to get to sleep.

Although I doubt that she set out to do so, Elizabeth Silverthorne writes terrific bedtime stories. To rate as terrific, a bedtime story must meet several criteria. First, it has to be interesting enough that you don't immediately slip-slide to the last letter of the alphabet (i.e., to the Z), while at the same time not be so riveting that Mr. Sand Man can't creep up and make a hit. Second, a bedtime story must be comforting. We all have to face a scary and unpredictable world out there. Why, for goodness sake, would you want to sharpen the focus on that scariness by reading a Stephen King book right before you go to sleep? Oh, no, you want to read a story that temporarily smoothes off those jagged edges and points the way to Sleepy Town. Most important, a bedtime story must be written clearly and well, so that strong visual images and pleasant word rhythms perfuse the creative, non-dominant side of your brain.

Elizabeth Silverthorne's books fill all the criteria. Her book *Legends and Lore of Texas Wildflowers* is especially comforting because indirectly it reminds us about the perennial predictability of Nature. This is particularly reassuring when the time has come to surrender the day's wakefulness. She even infuses sly bits of humor. Writing about the bluebonnet, whose spring arrival she describes as "the time when the sky seems to fall on Texas," she says, "The sight of bluebonnet fields has inspired countless painters and photographers, as well as poets and songwriters—with varying degrees of success."

Elizabeth Silverthorne's
FOOD ON TEXAS PLANTATIONS

Growing up in South Texas, eighteen miles from the Gulf of Mexico, I was only dimly aware that several large sugar cane and cotton plantations once had existed in the area. Many years later while doing research for *Plantation Life in Texas,* I discovered what life had been like for the early planter families in Texas—both white and black.

In the big house, huge fireplaces covered one wall of the kitchen. Iron cranes, equipped with S-shaped pot hooks, swiveled so the pots could be moved to hotter or cooler positions. Most of the cooking was done over hot coals which were raked out onto the hearthstones. Large pieces of meat were cooked on roasting spits held by firedogs (andirons).

Some kitchens had ovens (which were called Dutch ovens) built into the chimney to the side of the fireplace. A fire was built right in the oven, and when it had burned to coals, they were scraped out and the food placed inside.

Large, deep cast-iron pots, also called Dutch ovens, with rimmed lids and four little legs, were favorite cooking vessels. Another favorite was the spider, which had a long handle and three legs and resembled a skillet with a cover. Each of these was set directly over hot coals, with more coals piled on the rimmed lid. A good cook could prepare almost anything in a Dutch oven or a spider: breads, biscuits, potatoes, meats, soups and stews, pies and cakes.

In stark contrast to the abundant equipment in the planters' kitchens, the meager supply of pots and pans in the slaves' quarters allowed only simple, basic cooking. Most of their cooking was done outdoors, and families often had to eat from a common dish because of a lack of tableware.

Planters, like other early pioneers into Texas, made use of the plentiful gifts of nature. In the spring, after wild turkeys had gorged themselves on wild onions and cayenne peppers, there was a saying that they were already seasoned and needed only to be cleaned and roasted. Deer meat was ripened or aged by allowing it to hang from four days to two weeks. If the deer was full grown, the meat was marinated in a sauce that might include onion, carrot, celery, parsley, thyme, bay leaf, whole cloves, and vinegar. This marinade not only took away some of the gamy taste of the wild animal, but also tenderized it. Then the venison was larded with salt pork, roasted slowly, and basted frequently with the drippings. A tart red jelly often was served with it.

Small birds such as quail, snipe, partridge, and plover were cleaned and trussed, larded and roasted. They might be served on toast or alone with a gravy to which currant jelly had been added. They also were made into tasty pies. The cook placed the birds in a deep earthen dish; seasoned them with salt, pepper and butter and dredged them with flour. After adding cold water to nearly cover them, she topped them with a crust and baked them slowly until they were done. Wild ducks and blackbirds also were made into pies.

Plantation dwellers who lived near the Gulf of Mexico ate enormous quantities of oysters and crabs. On plantations located near rivers or lakes, both whites and blacks enjoyed fishing. The whole population sometimes turned out to fish and have a big fish fry, which included hush puppies made from cornmeal and fried in the same pan after the fish were done.

Pork was by far the most prevalent meat on Texas plantations. At hog butchering time there was an orgy of eating fresh pork and feasting on chitterlings, commonly called "chitlins." These are sections of the small intestines that have been cleaned, soaked in saltwater, boiled until tender, dipped in cornmeal, and fried crisp. Cracklings were another much-appreciated byproduct of hog butchering. They are the solid bits left when the lard of the hog is rendered or melted by heating. Slaves and white children loved to eat them as they were strained from the pot, but white adults usually preferred their cracklings mixed into corn bread batter to make "cracklin' bread."

It would be hard to exaggerate the importance of corn to these early settlers. Raising corn often was a matter of life or death. On plantations, the white and black families watched the corn crop, eagerly anticipating the first tender roasting ears. When the corn got too hard for roasting ears, it was ground into cornmeal. The earliest crops were ground by pounding the ears in a hollowed-out tree stump. Eventually there were gristmills on nearly every large plantation, but before that, slaves ground the corn on hand mills.

After the cornmeal was mixed with water and a little salt, it could be made into corn bread in a variety of ways. For ashcake, it was placed between dampened leaves and covered with hot ashes. For johnnycake, it was placed in a greased skillet and set over hot coals. In the field, placed on a hoe blade used as a griddle, it became hoecake. Cooked in a spider, it was corn pone or corn dodgers. An old recipe for corn pone reads: Mix 1 cup cornmeal, $\frac{1}{2}$ teaspoon salt, and 1 teaspoon sugar together. Stir in boiling water until thick enough to form patties. Make patties little larger than 4-bit [fifty-cent] pieces. Brown in hog lard.

Hominy, made by cooking the grains of corn in a weak solution of lye water, was a popular food. After the kernels swelled and shed their skins, they were washed repeatedly and boiled in two or three changes of water. Then, baked, boiled, or fried, hominy appeared often as a side dish on the planters' table. For breakfast, dried hominy was ground and served as grits.

Sweetening was obtained in several forms. Bee trees could be robbed of their honey, but the hives kept on many plantations were a surer source. Sorghum and sugarcane provided molasses and sugar. The slaves called syrup "long sweetening" and sugar "short sweetening." Their sweetening was more often long than short. Bought sugar came in loaves and had to be pulverized to use in cooking. Cake recipes were handed down from generation to generation and copied by hand in notebooks. Loaf cake was one favorite. A recipe that made "four large loaves" called for "two cups of butter, five of sugar, two of sour milk, eight of flour, one teaspoonful of saleratus [baking soda], six eggs, flavor to taste." Usually directions were not given for baking time or pan size, for each cook had her favorite utensils and knew how long the batter in them needed to bake.

Although coffee beans were expensive, it took oceans of strong black coffee to run a plantation. Fifteen to twenty cups a day was not considered an unusual amount for an individual to drink. The green coffee beans had to be roasted or parched on the hearth before they were ground in a coffee mill. The cooking method was simple: a handful of grounds was tossed into a pot of cold water that was set over hot coals to boil. After the coffee had boiled sufficiently, a few spoons of cold water settled the grounds, and the potent brew was ready to drink. When coffee was scarce, slaves drank coffee substitutes made out of whatever was available, including dried okra, potato peelings, wheat grains, and cornmeal.

Planters made wine from native mustang grapes. In addition to persimmon beer, individual plantations specialized in various beers made from sorghum juice and from grains such as rice and corn. Corn also could be made into a potent whisky and sugarcane into a strong rum. Honey and water were converted into mead, a smooth amber beverage popular in Europe as far back as written history goes. In the late spring or early summer, when dandelions matured, their blossoms could be picked and made into a light wine.

Preserving the harvest of fruits and vegetables was of the utmost importance if the planter and his family and slaves were to eat well during the winter. Much of the produce was stored in earth food mounds, in barns, or in cribs, but most of it was preserved by the women of the plantation. Many fruits and vegetables could be dried—either in the sun or by the fireplace. As the dried food was put away, chinaberry leaves were placed between layers to discourage insects and worms. Beans, peas, pumpkins, sweet potatoes, corn, okra, peaches, figs, and pears all could be enjoyed dried. Peach leather was a delicious way of saving fresh peaches to use in peach dumplings, cobblers, and other dishes. Ripe peaches were mashed and the pulp spread about a half-inch thick and dried for a few days. When it was leathery, it was rolled or folded and put away for future use. Pickling was another means of preservation. Watermelon rinds, tomatoes, cabbages, cucumbers, and the feet of hogs were among the many foods pickled in solutions of salt, vinegar, and spices and enjoyed during the winter season.

Strings of dried red peppers decorated the kitchens, as did bunches of herbs. Next to the kitchen on every sizable plantation grew an herb garden fragrant with mint, sage, parsley, thyme, and savory. And most plantation mistresses observed the old rhyme about these seasonings: "Cut herbs just as the dew does dry. Tie them loosely and hang them high."

Between Christmas Eve and New Year's Day, plantation families took turns hosting dinners, supper, parties, and dances. Eggnog and syllabub were the popular drinks of the season. As early as Christmas of 1843, William Bollaert, who was traveling in Texas, celebrated (perhaps too well), for he mentions egg nog as the "favourite beverage" of the day, "made of the white and yellow of eggs, beaten up separately, the yellow with sugar, then both mixed with whiskey, brandy and new milk to thin it—somewhat pleasant, but of a bilious nature."

Syllabub, a lighter mixture of eggs, milk, wine, and spices, sometimes was eaten as a custard with a spoon but more often was drunk from fine glass goblets. Since it contained wine instead of whiskey, syllabub was considered a better drink for ladies.

Although slaves seldom shared the rich variety of meats, breads, vegetables, fruits, jams, jellies, and desserts they prepared for the planters' tables, many of them remembered fresh, abundant food as one of the pleasures of their dreary lives on the plantations. Pragmatic masters fed their slaves well, not only to keep them strong and to prevent illness, but also to keep them contented. In their extreme old age, many former slaves still remembered the pleasure of eating roasting ears of corn, sweet potatoes, and corn pone cooked in the hot embers of a fireplace; savoring molasses poured over hot corn bread; eating hog jowls and greens, chitlin's, cracklings, souse (hog's head cheese), and a favorite dish of baked opossum in a ring of sweet potatoes swimming in molasses.

Bountiful plantation hospitality dictated that a lavish array of dishes appear before guests. Before he was president, Rutherford B. Hayes visited several Texas plantations and noted in his journal: "The Texans are essentially carnivorous. Pork ribs, pigs' feet, veal beef (grand), chickens, venison and dried meat frequently seen on the table at once." Hunks of pork were used for flavoring all kinds of peas, beans and greens. Gravies and sauces were rich and creamy. Chopped suet was used in many recipes for puddings and other desserts. Cakes and pies were loaded with large amounts of lard, butter, eggs, sugar, and cream. Obviously, calories, cholesterol, and saturated fat were unknown quantities in the high days of Texas plantation living, and certainly never again will we sit down to such prodigious feasts of unadulterated, homegrown, fresh-tasting foods.

BOOKS

The Ghost of Padre Island. Nashville, Tenn.: Abingdon Press, 1975.

First Ladies of Texas. Belton, Tex.: Stillhouse Hollow Press, 1976.

I, Heracles. Nashville, Tenn.: Abingdon Press, 1978.

Ashbel Smith of Texas. College Station: Texas A&M University Press, 1982.

Plantation Life in Texas. College Station: Texas A&M University Press, 1986.

Marjorie Kinnan Rawlings: Sojourner at Cross Creek. Woodstock, N.Y.: Overlook Press, 1988.

Christmas in Texas. College Station: Texas A&M University Press, 1990.

Fiesta! Brookfield, Conn.: Millbook Press, 1992.

Sarah Orne Jewett. Woodstock, N.Y.: Overlook Press, 1993.

Legends and Lore of Texas Wildflowers. College Station: Texas A&M University Press, 1996.

Women Pioneers in Texas Medicine (with Geneva Fulgham). College Station: Texas A&M University Press, 1997.

Mary Willis Walker

Mary Willis Walker, one of the best-known mystery writers from Texas, sets her stories in Austin. In 1994, she won the coveted Edgar award for best first mystery novel.

Mary Willis Walker

Back where I come from, we take the word *crude* to mean unrefined or tasteless, maybe even vulgar. For that reason, you can understand why I fretted for days after a book reviewer for the *Houston Chronicle* described the hand-drawn maps in my first book as "crude." Crude? Simple, maybe, but not *crude.* Finally, I looked up the word in the dictionary. It's true that *crude* can mean *unrefined,* but it can also mean *unadorned.* I immediately felt better.

If I were Mary Willis Walker, I might have fretted for days after a book reviewer praised—of all things—a grisly buzzard scene in *The Red Scream:* "Walker has written the best buzzard scene in the history of the printed word." Instead, Ms. Walker was delighted. This is because she has a special place in her heart (or, perhaps, spleen or liver or eye sockets) for these birds. In fact, all of her books have scenes starring buzzards.

She explains it this way: "I feel an affinity for them because they are the consummate scavengers. They take roadkill that no one else wants to get near and they eat it and turn it into energy for the most beautiful soaring flight. As a writer, I feel that I am in that same business. Like a buzzard, I am also a scavenger, cruising the highway, looking for some juicy roadkill. I live my life always the opportunist watching for juicy morsels to feed my writing habit, to lend energy to my stories, to get them off the ground. And I'm not fussy where I get those morsels."

I'm not sure I've ever heard it put quite that crudely. I mean that as a compliment, because Ms. Walker is giving us unadorned truth: for story ideas, all writers must lay aside their squeamishness and become opportunistic scavengers.

Mary Willis Walker's
BREAST OF CHICKEN A L'ORANGE

The real tragedy of middle age is a sluggish metabolism, says Molly Cates, the protagonist of *The Red Scream* and *Under the Beetle's Cellar*. I'm afraid I have to agree with her, and for writers—alas!—the problem is even worse. After a day of intense labor, you feel you've earned the right to eat like a lumberjack, but, unfortunately, you've done nothing more physical than move your fingertips up and down on a keyboard, an activity which consumes maybe five calories per chapter—max.

So a low-fat diet is my fate. And yours, too, most likely. But that doesn't mean we can't eat well.

Here is a recipe with many virtues: it is low in fat, simple (despite the French name), quick, and delicious. My children ask for it from time to time when they remember that long ago, before I got obsessed with writing, I used to cook real food for them.

Ingredients
8 chicken breasts, boned and skinned (Don't do it yourself—
   buy them that way!)
$\frac{1}{2}$ cup flour
2 tsp. salt
1 tsp. paprika
3 tbs. nonfat margarine (This recipe originally called for $\frac{1}{2}$ cup
   butter, but it tastes almost as good without it.)
2 cups orange juice
1 lb. sliced mushrooms (or more, if you really love mushrooms)
Garnish of toasted nuts, avocado, orange, or grapefruit slices.

Dust chicken lightly with mixture of flour, salt, and paprika. Sauté in margarine on medium heat until golden brown, tossing mushrooms in toward the end. Add orange juice, cover, and simmer for 15 minutes, basting once or twice. Uncover and reduce liquid to a slightly thickened sauce.

If you care about making it looking pretty, you can stand the breasts up around a heap of rice or pasta, pour the sauce over it, and decorate with avocado or nuts or orange and grapefruit sections.

This recipe works out every single time, and it's even better the next day—a claim you cannot make for many things in this world.

Note: A version of this recipe appeared in *Helen Corbitt Cooks for Company* (Boston: Houghton Mifflin, 1974).

BOOKS

Zero at the Bone. New York: St. Martin's, 1991; Toronto: Worldwide, 1993; New York: Bantam, 1997.

The Red Scream. Garden City, N.Y.: Doubleday, 1994; New York: Bantam, 1995.

Under the Beetle's Cellar. Garden City, N.Y.: Doubleday, 1995; New York: Bantam, 1996.

Roland H. Wauer retired from the U.S. National Park Service after thirty-two years of service as a ranger, interpreter, biologist, and chief of resource management. He is the well-informed author of numerous field guides.

Roland H. Wauer

I have spent more time with Ro Wauer than with all the contributors to this book combined. We have spent many hours in the early morning light, whispering excitedly to one another, followed by earnest, searching moments of silence. At times, we would be so close that we could hear each others' quickening breath and feel the heat from each others' bodies as first one of us and then the other would gush, "Yes! Oh, yes. There it is. A Colima warbler. Yes!"

There's hardly anything that I would rather do than go for long walks and look at birds, and there is no one on God's green earth that I would rather go birding with than Ro Wauer. Former chief naturalist for the National Park Service, Ro has forgotten more about birds and all manner of other nature-related topics than most of us will ever learn. (Ro, that is a manner of speech which is meant as a compliment, not an observation about creeping senility. I want you to know that. Far be it from me to mention that you sometimes take a moment to remember the name of a wildflower.) He is also good-humored, energetic, well-read, and articulate. These are exceedingly desirable traits in someone that you plan to hike with for many hours. And, for that matter, whisper excitedly with.

Roland H. Wauer's

FLYING SHRIMP FRIED RICE

Shrimp fried rice is a recipe that I got from my mother. She once won a county bake-off or some other local contest with it when she was a young woman in Utah. And it is one of my earliest food memories. As a kid growing up in Idaho, a long, long way from where shrimp occur naturally, my mother's shrimp fried rice was a winner. It had that "stove-top stuffing" appeal that enticed me home to the dinner table from whatever else I might have been doing at the time. So it was only natural that shrimp fried rice became a recipe of choice during my bachelor years, after I escaped from academia.

Not until many years later, however, after acquiring real shrimp on the Texas Gulf coast, did I truly appreciate the gourmet quality of shrimp fried rice. For all those years when I lived in the Intermountain West and the Greater Southwest, the shrimp utilized in my shrimp fried rice recipe was derived from frozen stock, purchased at the local grocery. In retrospect, I suspect that most, if not all, of that had been packaged and frozen months or even years earlier and rarely reached two on a ten-scale of taste. But, after moving to Victoria, near the Texas Gulf coast, suddenly, out of the blue, I was able to purchase fresh shrimp, caught only hours before and never frozen. Taste jumped dramatically into the upper range, and so did my shrimp fried rice. No longer was I forced to use soggy, chlorine-tasting gobs of seafood; I could have the real thing. It was like comparing Roseanne with Cheryl Tiegs or Jerry Jones with Tom Landry.

Then along comes my friend Deborah with her super idea of a cookbook featuring recipes by Texas authors. And she has the gall to suggest that I submit a recipe using some kind of bird, instead of shrimp. Just because I happen to be an avid birder and our friendship is based on birding, she expects me to come up with something that flies rather than swims. I tried! I do make pretty good turkey enchiladas, but lots of other folks do, too. I even tried using emu sausage but decided I couldn't afford that. And I tried chocolate chicken wings, but they tasted more like chicken covered with chocolate than the popular, crunchy, ever-so-delicious, chocolate-covered grasshoppers. And so shrimp fried rice won the day! But to make a major concession, I have renamed my shrimp fried rice recipe "Flying Shrimp Fried Rice."

By now, I am sure that if any readers are still with me, you are anxious to learn about my (my mother's) prize-winning dish of shrimp fried rice. But first a caveat: if you want the real taste, use all the right ingredients and do it right. Don't take any shortcuts, like using frozen shrimp or precooked rice.

Here are the ingredients:
3 cups of long-grain rice
3 cups of fresh medium-sized shrimp
6 fresh green onions (scallions)
1 green bell pepper
5 eggs (fried)
1 stick of butter
2 tbs. Worcestershire sauce
1 tsp. salt
$\frac{1}{2}$ tsp. pepper

Here are your instructions:
Cook rice to dry; don't use if moist and gooey. Using a large pan, such as an electric skillet, melt the butter and fry the green pepper until lightly browned. Then add sauce, salt, and pepper. Add rice and cook for $\frac{1}{2}$ hour on low heat (stir occasionally). Then add sliced precooked eggs, shrimp, and chopped onions (stir occasionally). Let this whole mess cook for another $\frac{1}{2}$ hour on low heat. It is now ready to eat!

Some folks like to add moderate amounts of soy sauce. Others, usually those West Texas types who rarely eat in restaurants, like a hot chili or two on the side.

And if this meal doesn't really satisfy your appetite, you can go back to soggy fried shrimp and emu burgers.

BOOKS

Naturalist's Big Bend. College Station: Texas A&M University Press, 1980.

Naturalist's Mexico. College Station: Texas A&M University Press, 1992.

Visitor's Guide to the Birds of the Eastern National Parks, U.S. and Canada. Santa Fe, N.M.: John Muir Publications, 1992.

Visitor's Guide to the Birds of the Rocky Mountain National Parks. Santa Fe, N.M.: John Muir Publications, 1993.

Visitor's Guide to the Birds of the Central National Parks, U.S. and Canada. Santa Fe, N.M.: John Muir Publications, 1994.

A Birder's West Indies: An Island-by-Island Tour. Austin: University of Texas Press, 1996.

A Field Guide to Birds of the Big Bend. Houston: Gulf Publishers, 1996.

Birds of Zion National Park and Vicinity. Logan: Utah State University Press, 1997.

For All Seasons: A Big Bend Journal. Austin: University of Texas Press, 1997.

Bryan Woolley grew up in Fort Davis and currently writes for the Dallas Morning News. *He is the author of numerous works of fiction and nonfiction.*

Bryan Woolley

Occasionally I will read something that I wish—oh, God, how I wish—that I had written. I think, "Those are my words. He found them first, but those are my words." I am so awestruck, and, okay, I'll admit it, so envious of the writer's handling of the subject that it makes my lower molars hurt. Nearly every time I read something that Bryan Woolley has written, my lower molars hurt. It is somehow fitting that his is the last chapter in this book, because, of all the writers included (and, folks, these are some of our state's best), Mr. Woolley's writing style is the one that I admire the most.

Reading one of Bryan Woolley's stories is like watching a world-class gymnast on television. As the athlete flawlessly performs the routine, you can't imagine that he was born to do anything else but gymnastics. This is because he has practiced so much, has paid such careful attention to every detail, and has put so much of his heart into the craft that he makes all those twisting somersaults and double back flips look easy. So deceptively easy, in fact, that you find yourself thinking, "I believe I'll just step out in the front yard and try a couple of those." However, until you heave yourself up off the couch, take a running start, and end up in traction, you will never know how very, very difficult it is to make it all look so easy.

The gymnast is also joyful. Even when the background music is somber, there is an oh-boy-this-is-fun liveliness in his movements. So, too, it is with Mr. Woolley's writing. Beneath his words—even if those words make you cry—you sense his enthusiasm about the subject. Fueling this enthusiasm are two personality traits: curiosity and, more important, compassion. It is that combination, I suspect, that begets the words that make my lower molars hurt.

With that, I close.

Bryan Woolley
GOD'S OWN PIMENTO CHEESE

Whenever my grandmother would send me down to Clara Johnson's store for a jar of pimentos, I knew she was going to take me and my younger brothers and sisters on a picnic. I would run to the store and get the precious little jar and maybe a big sack of potato chips, and by the time I got back Mommy, as we called her, already would be grating a big hunk of cheddar. She would hack up the pimentos, throw them in a bowl with the grated cheese, spoon in a couple of gobs of mayonnaise and mash it all together with a fork. Then she would smear the mixture on slices of light bread, slap more slices on top and wrap the sandwiches in wax paper. With the potato chips, a jar of pickles, some apples and a couple of cartons of Dr. Pepper, the six of us would pile into the Plymouth and drive out to Point of Rock, a huge jumble of boulders a few miles out of Fort Davis, and spend the afternoon climbing on the rocks and chasing each other.

I still love pimento cheese, as much for the memories it evokes as for the taste of it.

Here's an improved version of my grandmother's delicacy, which I stole from Reynolds Price. I've added a few touches of my own.

Grate a pound or more of the sharpest cheddar cheese you can find. Coarsely chop one jar of pimentos and one or two cloves of garlic. If you like jalapeños, chop up one or two and throw them in, too. Mix into the grated cheese, adding lots of freshly ground pepper and just a little salt. Gradually add enough good mayonnaise to form a stiff, chunky paste, but not enough to make it gooey. I like to add a dollop of lemon juice, and, if you're not going with the jalapeños, you might want to shake in a mite of Tabasco. But not enough to knock out the taste of the cheese and other stuff. Smear generously on bread—the darker and grainier the better—and have at it. It's also great on flour tortillas.

Hop in the Plymouth and drive to Point of Rock. Don't be in a hurry to get back.

BOOKS

Some Sweet Day. New York: Random House, 1974; El Paso: Texas Western Press, 1996.

We Be Here When the Morning Comes. Lexington: University Press of Kentucky, 1975.

Time and Place. New York: Dutton, 1977; Fort Worth: Texas Christian University Press, 1985.

November 22. New York: Seaview, 1981.

Sam Bass. San Antonio, Tex.: Corona, 1983.

The Time of My Life. Bryan, Tex.: Shearer, 1984.

Where Texas Meets the Sea. Dallas: Pressworks, 1985.

The Edge of the West. El Paso: Texas Western Press, 1990.

The Bride Wore Crimson. El Paso: Texas Western Press, 1993.

Generations. El Paso: Texas Western Press, 1996.

Recipe Index